Rage and Reason
Women Playwrights
on Playwriting

Rage and Reason
Women Playwrights
on Playwriting

Heidi Stephenson
and Natasha Langridge

METHUEN DRAMA

Published by Methuen

First published in the United Kingdom in 1997 by Methuen,
Random House; 20 Vauxhall Bridge Road, London SW1V 2SA

Random House Australia (Pty) Limited
20 Alfred Street, Milsons Point, Sydney,
New South Wales 2061, Australia

Random House New Zealand Limited
18 Poland Road, Glenfield
Auckland 10, New Zealand

Random House South Africa (Pty) Limited
Endulini, 5A Jubilee Road, Parktown 2193, South Africa

Random House UK Limited Reg. No. 954009
A CIP catalogue record for this book
is available from the British Library

ISBN 0 413 71600 7

Phototypeset in Stempel Garamond and Frutiger Light by Intype London Ltd
Printed and bound in Great Britain by
Mackays of Chatham PLC, Chatham, Kent

For William Stephenson,
Mary-Ellen, Anny, Jayne and Crub.

Contents

Many thanks to the following people for their invaluable assistance:

Leigh Acton, Thomas Albrecht, Claire Armistead (at the *Guardian*), Ilse Axer, Phil Beadle, Michael Billington (at the *Guardian*), Sebastian Born (at The Agency), Jack Bradley (at the Royal National Theatre), Mike Bradwell (at the Bush Theatre), Peggy Butcher (at Faber & Faber), Leah Byrne, Annie Castledine, Chris, Regina and Helga (at Smallbrook House), Emma Cook (at the *Independent*), Stephen Daldry (at the Royal Court Theatre), Lucy Davies (at the Donmar Warehouse), Romano Decker, Dominic Dromgoole (at the Old Vic), Ellen Dryden, Sue Ellis, Trina Epsom (at MacNaughton Lord Representation), Richard Eyre (at the Royal National Theatre), Vicky Featherstone (at Paines Plough), Elisabeth Feuser, Karyn Fletcher, Lisa Goldman (at The Red Room), Bonnie Greer, Dave Hall, Rod Hall (at A. P. Watt), Sally Homer, Mark Ingarfield, Ben Jankovich (at Hampstead Theatre), Joanna and Tony (formerly at the Brix Theatre), Jude Kelly (at West Yorkshire Playhouse), Jacqueline Korn (at David Higham Associates), Goran Kostic, Julia Kreitman (at The Agency), Kristine Landon-Smith (at Tamasha), Sheila Lemon (at The Agency), Jenny Long (at the Theatre Managers Association), Nick Marston (at A. P. Watt), Judy Martin, Ruth Needham (at MBA Literary Agents), Pamela Osborne, Emily Pinkney, Alan Radcliffe (at William Morris Agency), Joanne Reardon (at the Bush Theatre), Samantha, Leah Schmidt, Brian Schwartz (at Off-Stage), Sheffield Academic Press, Max Stafford-Clark (at Out of Joint), Sarah Stroud (at Judy Daish Associates), Jenny Topper (at Hampstead Theatre), Richard Wareham, Colin Watkeys, Susanna Wilford, Jules Wright (at the Women's Playhouse Trust) and Graham Wybrow (at the Royal Court Theatre). With special thanks to Michael Earley and Helena Beynon (at Methuen), Mel Kenyon (at Casarotto Ramsay), Geraldine Collinge (at BAC), the staff at the Theatre Museum, Covent Garden and, of course, to the playwrights themselves – without whom this book would have been just a passing dream.

Introduction

British theatre, in the last thirty years, has undergone nothing short of a revolution – from a point where the woman playwright was almost an anomaly, to the present, in which more women are writing for the stage than ever before. Never have we had such a prolific and diverse body of their dramatic work as we do now. Many of their plays, like Caryl Churchill's *Top Girls* and *Cloud Nine*, Pam Gems's *Dusa, Fish, Stas and Vi*, Charlotte Keatley's *My Mother Said I Never Should*, Sarah Daniels's *Masterpieces*, Timberlake Wertenbaker's *Our Country's Good* and Sarah Kane's *Blasted*, have swiftly become canonical and are now contemporary landmarks by consensus. Women playwrights have broadened the agenda of British drama. Both the form and content of their work have pushed the boundaries of what it is possible to show and tell on stage and our theatre culture is infinitely richer for their contribution. We felt their titanic achievements needed celebrating. We were also curious to discover more about how they craft their plays, why they write, where they find their stories and why, despite their success, they continue to be under-represented in mainstream theatre.

That they are under-represented is acknowledged by theatre managements across the board in Britain. The simple fact is that theatre is still predominantly run by men and commented on by men. The most up-to-date research, Jenny Long's survey 'What Share of the Cake Now?'* concludes that only twenty per cent of productions

*This survey, conducted at the end of 1994, which analyses the distribution patterns of employment amongst women in theatre companies in receipt of Arts Council revenue funding in England, is the only current statistical research available, but from our own investigations, its results still hold true. The author, Jenny Long, works for the Theatre Managers Association, who are planning to publish the survey. The analysis was undertaken as a graduate thesis at the University of North London.

are by women and that the figure drops to fourteen per cent in companies where the artistic director is male. Long's findings also reveal that women playwrights, proportionally, are less well represented the larger the size of the theatre and the larger the share of the revenue grant. In building-based companies, a marked decrease has been recorded in the number of main-house productions by them, with an increase in studio productions.

When we started this project, the problem was exacerbated by a phase of 'lads' plays. Britain's powerhouses of new writing, and most notably the Royal Court Theatre, were presenting a seemingly endless barrage of male-orientated work like Tracy Letts's *Killer Joe*, Louis Mellis and David Scinto's *Gangster No 1*, Jez Butterworth's *Mojo*, David Greer's *Burning Blue*, Simon Bent's *Goldhawk Road*, Kieron Carney's *Afters*, Patrick Marber's *Dealer's Choice*, Paul Hodson's stage adaptation of Nick Hornby's *Fever Pitch*, Irvine Welsh's *Trainspotting*, William Gaminara's *According to Hoyle*, Jonathan Lewis's *Our Boys* and Simon Block's *Not A Game For Boys*. These plays, which were also often sadly misogynistic, gained a very high profile. What might our women playwrights say about the dominance of and vogue for the work of the male playwright? What might they say about the state of the art or the theatre at large? Did they feel beleaguered or were they optimistic? The title, *Rage and Reason: Women Playwrights on Playwriting*, emerged as a result of this debate.

The selection process was difficult. From an initial list of seventy-four names, we had to nominate twenty, so that those interviewed would be given the space to express their views. Our main aim was to give a solid sampling of the spectrum of writers whose work is seen in Britain, from the well-established like Pam Gems, Timberlake Wertenbaker and Sharman Macdonald, to the lesser known, like Tanika Gupta (who at the time of her interview was still unproduced). We wanted as diverse a range as possible: writers who scale the heights of the Royal National Theatre and the West End, writers from the Fringe and outside London, performer-writers, young writers and those who started their careers in the sixties and seventies. We chose them because of the vitality and ingenuity of their work and because they each have a unique slant on playwriting, theatre and society.

To retain as much of each playwright's personality and voice as possible, the interviews are deliberately conversational. All the writers discuss their plays and the myriad of themes and issues which interest them with extraordinary openness and honesty. What we have as a result is a privileged, deeply personal and fascinating insight into their (very different) creative and political thinking. They have put themselves on the line. While not all the playwrights believe that gender or under-representation are central issues, there is general agreement that their work is being marginal-ised. Most of the writers also believe that national theatre critics not only frequently approach their plays with preconceived ideas, but that the current methods and criteria of theatre criticism are often inadequate. On the face of it there appears to be an uncon-scious prejudice, which doesn't feel that unconscious if, as Winsome Pinnock points out, you happen to be a woman playwright. But the reasons for it are complex and, as Timberlake Wertenbaker says, 'hard to untangle'.

* * *

The task of managing theatres and making programming decisions in these financially difficult times is, Clare McIntyre concedes, 'a deadly one' and unless playwrights operate self-sufficiently, as both Claire Dowie and Debbie Isitt have chosen to do by producing their own work, women playwrights find themselves in the hands of the people making those decisions. Whether or not their work gets staged depends on what theatre managements want at the time. Timberlake Wertenbaker mentions the fact that during the mid-eighties the work of women playwrights, especially under Max Stafford-Clark's artistic directorship at the Royal Court, was in demand, 'it was a time when women were prominent,' but that then 'there was a certain reaction in the press and suddenly they were hungry for a different kind of play: male violence and homo-erotica'. The progress towards a more equal balance of male and female work which had been made (Max Stafford-Clark recalls that thirty-eight per cent of his output was by women writers) took a downward turn. 'Women writers who were prominent in the eighties were knocked out,' says Vicky Featherstone, artistic director of Paines Plough, who also believes, (as does Max Stafford-Clark), that there's been a 'feminist theatre backlash'.

Stephen Daldry, the out-going artistic director of the Royal Court, suggests that the plays of many women writers are not perhaps 'capturing the zeitgeist of fashion. Women as an issue on its own' or 'work within the context of feminism is unfashionable', he says. He admits his personal taste does not favour plays which focus on 'Oh, what happened to socialism? Reflective, wistful plays about the end of an era,' but adds that this has nothing to do with gender. 'It's about men and women, a certain age group of writers' and that aside of this, 'The building is not run on my taste.' He is keen to point out that 'Statistically speaking, the Royal Court in the last three years has produced more women playwrights than ever in its history'. But he admits that the figures are somewhat distorted because the Royal Court is also now producing more new plays than ever before and concedes, 'No. We don't put on enough women'.

Mike Bradwell, artistic director of the Bush Theatre, believes that women playwrights are battling a false perception that their work is 'breast-beating, worthy or proselytising' (a negation of the wonderful humour, energy and originality of their work) and that their plays have become identified with 'an "ism". Something you do and once you've managed to identify and ghettoise it, you don't have to think about it.' The media's promotion of a 'post-feminist' era has probably not helped matters, giving theatre managements licence to drop their guard against an over-emphasis of the male dramatic voice. But it seems ridiculous to consider women playwrights either fashionable or not. Gone are the days when their focus was principally on 'women's issues' – although rape, surrogacy, pornography and mother-child relationships, some of the subjects commonly explored in plays by women, were hardly of minority relevance or appeal. But women playwrights *have* branched out and though, like their male counterparts, they now often write smaller cast plays in the hope of getting them staged, the subjects they deal with – war, class, crime, fate, alienation, power, civilisation, identity – are not marginal, and the way in which they deal with them far from limited or outdated.

Timberlake Wertenbaker believes that one problem may be that plays by women on 'big' subjects are not always well-received. It's an issue that Phyllis Nagy also feels strongly about, that it's harder for 'big' plays to get on when they're written by a woman and that for too long women's plays that were 'allowed' and encouraged were 'all about the process of being a woman, as filtered through the eyes of men'. What conformed to a male artistic director's notion of what women should be interested in got on, she says, and there's been a resistance to everything else.

Bryony Lavery cites her lack of mainstream success (although the mainstream is not something she particularly admires or aspires to) as having a lot to do with the fact that as a lesbian woman, she cannot be 'deemed to hold central the hopes and fears of humanity'. As Naomi Wallace points out, universality is still seen as white, male and straight, and Pam Gems feels that we've actually slipped back where women writers and universality is concerned. Their work is not yet 'seen as a metaphor in the sense that if we go and see *Hamlet* we don't think, "This is just an adolescent play for men who feel a bit lost," ' says Charlotte Keatley. 'We think "This play is a metaphor for all of us." ' She believes that this 'will change just by having more plays by women'. 'I think a lot of directors have a very uncomprehensive view of what playwriting can be and what theatre can be,' says Dominic Dromgoole, director of new plays at London's Old Vic, 'and so you tend to get a limited range of enthusiasm. The reason they put boys plays on is because they only see the world as a boy's world. They read a play by a woman and they don't get it.' He emphasises that this is not through lack of goodwill though.

As Sarah Daniels points out, however, theatres in receipt of public subsidy 'have an obligation to produce new work which reflects a cross-section of themes about different experiences in society'. This has nothing to do with 'political correctness or positive discrimination', she says, 'but fairness.' She draws attention to the Royal National Theatre which 'does have the word "national" in the title – so where is half the population?' And where are the black and Asian writers? 'It would be exciting if we could just see what's happening in society reflected on stage,' says Winsome Pinnock. But 'it's not fashionable to ask, "Why haven't you got any women writers?" ' says April de Angelis, and 'You don't want to force quotas because it should be in spirit that they want to give women writers a voice.'

Richard Eyre, the out-going artistic director of the Royal National Theatre, says that if the appropriate scripts were there, he would put them on. 'Believe me, if you run a theatre you *long* for a script. It doesn't matter if it's written by a giraffe – if it's good you want to do it.' He says he 'honestly can't think of a single example of a play by a woman which is generally agreed by readers of mixed gender to be good which hasn't got on', adding that where the National Theatre's main Olivier stage is concerned, Eyre has been 'trying for nearly ten years to get new writing to put on', but that 'there are very few plays that have been robust enough'.

Commercial considerations, as Richard Eyre admits, also come into the equation; raising the question of whether theatres perhaps view the work of women playwrights as more of a commercial risk. The National clearly has a problem on its hands with both the Lyttelton and Olivier stages, but why have so many plays by women, including plays by well-established playwrights found themselves Upstairs at the Royal Court and not on the main stage? Stephen Daldry says that practical obstacles to do with space and programming prevented the sold-out *Blasted* from transferring

Downstairs and that he felt Clare McIntyre's *The Thickness of Skin*, for example, was a 'fragile' play, better suited to the smaller space. 'I think you might find that some of the women's plays Downstairs haven't found a large, popular audience,' he says, 'but I would resist any challenge that we haven't therefore put them on Downstairs.'

But Pam Gems predominantly writes biographical plays now, partly because it's so much harder to get an original play produced. 'Everyone's concerned with bums on seats,' says Tanika Gupta. 'While literary managers might like my writing, artistic directors don't believe it's going to bring in the punters' – a notion she obviously challenges. 'Theatres are less prepared to take risks with women's work,' says Joanne Reardon, literary manager at the Bush. 'Their work is perceived as more of a risk generally.' As Mel Kenyon, literary agent at Casarotto Ramsay, points out, 'This deep-seated and erroneous perception not only debilitates female playwrights psychologically, but also has far-reaching financial repercussions. To be crude, the average commissioning fee is a few thousand and a play may take a year to write. If only produced in small spaces, no royalties accrue.'

Yet plays by women do achieve box-office success and are popular with audiences. Sheila Stephenson's *The Memory of Water* (a first stage play) played to ninety-eight per cent capacity at Hampstead. Diane Samuels's *Kindertransport* transferred to the West End after a recent revival. Sue Glover's *Bondagers* sold out at the Donmar Warehouse at the end of an extensive national tour. Yasmina Reza's *Art* has been a huge West End hit. Pam Gems's *Stanley* is currently on Broadway and Charlotte Keatley's *My Mother Said I Never Should* has been so commercially successful that it is still providing her with an adequate income ten years after it opened at the Royal Court.

Sarah Daniels believes there is too much emphasis on the new play having to be a success anyway, although she concedes that theatres do need to keep afloat. But such commercial considerations put a heavy burden on writers which has repercussions beyond the immediate play concerned. As Anna Reynolds says, if your first play is a hit, 'then great, but you've got to come up with another one very quickly. If you don't, or your second play is not as good or is different, or doesn't come for three years, then you can forget it.' Often the best work doesn't meet with instant commercial success and there clearly has to be some room for 'failure'. Anna Reynolds adds that although in general we've got more new plays now than ever before, it's at the expense of giving writers time to develop, which has long-term implications for the future of theatre.

Because we also live in such a fast-moving media age, as Charlotte
Keatley notes, everything, plays and playwrights included, gets
hurled aside for the next wave to come in and theatre doesn't work
well at this pace at all.

Theatre managements do have a point, however, when they say
that women do not currently submit the number of plays that men
do. Graham Whybrow, the Royal Court's literary manager, says
that out of a sample batch of scripts he looked at recently, only
189 out of 1000 were by women and that this necessarily means
that the ratio of work selected from them will be lower. Jenny
Topper, artistic director at Hampstead Theatre makes the same
point – although she believes things are 'shifting now', that more
plays by women are being submitted. The problem is partly to do
with 'a process of numbers', as Clare McIntyre acknowledges, but
number-crunching both is, and is not, at the heart of the matter.
The responsibility lies with theatres too. The theatre establishment
expends little energy, in real terms, to welcome new women writers
into the theatre or to value the more established playwrights. What
would inspire fledgling dramatists to submit plays when they see
the work of good, experienced female dramatists frequently being
undermined and undervalued, not only by critics, but by theatre
practitioners themselves? It's a self-fulfilling prophecy.

Things are opening up. London's Bush Theatre, which is now
identified as 'woman-friendly', currently have seven plays by
women in the pipeline, 'all of which we'll probably do,' says Mike
Bradwell, who has also commissioned Sarah Daniels, Rebecca Prit-
chard and Catherine Johnson 'simply because they are three of my
favourite writers'. Not coincidentally, Joanne Reardon cites that in
the last six months the number of plays she has received from
women has gone up significantly from twenty–thirty to forty per
cent. 'There are an enormous amount of women writing,' says
Dominic Dromgoole, a former Bush artistic director, 'and they're
writing some of the best work we have. They are generating their
own excitement and inspiring others to follow them.'

Women dramatists still need directors to champion their work
though. As Jack Bradley, formerly with the Soho Theatre Company
and now literary manager at the Royal National Theatre, points
out, it doesn't matter how enthusiastic his department get about a
play, if there's no director behind it, the likelihood is that it won't
go on. This problem is aggravated by the fact that women directors
frequently choose to stage the work of male playwrights or go with
the classics. There are women 'who don't particularly want to see
what women are writing', says Timberlake Wertenbaker, which she

suggests may be informed by culture as much as preference, but which has aided the marginalisation of the female voice in theatre. 'Women directors need to seek out and commit to women writers,' says Jules Wright, artistic director of the Women's Playhouse Trust. But women directors still 'get such an extraordinarily raw deal', says Lisa Goldman, artistic director of London Fringe theatre The Red Room, that this is sometimes made impossible. She believes that 'if there was an opening up of opportunity for them', we would 'see a change'. Charlotte Keatley adds that it doesn't help that directors are not given *auteur* status for directing a new play, which they get more readily with 'a wild interpretation of Marlowe'. On a challenging note, Richard Eyre offers that if directors Deborah Warner or Katie Mitchell 'wanted to direct a play by a woman' at the National Theatre, 'I'd put it on. They do have a position of strength,' he says.

Phyllis Nagy believes that the form of women playwrights' work has also contributed to their under-representation. Unlike most male playwrights who, she says, write 'thesis' plays, often asking rhetorical questions in the process, many women have moved away from the traditional and are writing plays which are an open-ended examination and employ sophisticated new structures, far from the linear, limited parameters of the 'well-made play'. Although not all women playwrights are 'genuine Picassos', as Sarah Daniels points out, some directors may be at a loss when it comes to seeing the quality, ingenuity and craft of these plays. Because this work sets a precedent, there may be an artistic fear about approaching it, or a belief that it wouldn't work. Playwrights have literally been told, 'This is not a play.'

In all the interviews critics come under considerable attack. The critic versus the artist is, of course, an age-old battle. Playwrights are naturally sensitive to being labelled, defined and judged and that is how critics frame reviews. In an age where a playwright's success is largely measured by critical approval and, closely linked to this, how well they do at the box-office, critics wield huge power. As Sarah Kane, who became an instant target of the word-war, points out, critics 'have the power to kill a show dead with their cynicism'. She regrets that they don't take their jobs as seriously as the writers 'they so frequently and casually try to destroy'. Fortunately, the critical vitriol levelled against *Blasted* (which was variously described as 'This disgusting feast of filth' and 'like having your face rammed into an over-flowing ashtray') didn't do it any damage at the box-office – in fact, the play became something of a *cause célèbre*. But such cases are an exception to the rule and bad reviews usually mean box-office death, which also seems to have a bearing on whether or not the future work of a writer gets staged and where it gets staged.

For women playwrights part of the problem, undoubtedly, is that the vast majority of critics are male and that the same critics have been in their posts for a very long time. As Michael Billington, the *Guardian's* chief theatre critic, says himself, 'We're conscious that we're like a portable version of the Garrick club. A bunch of middle-aged men' and that it 'would be healthier if there were a greater diversity of critics'. Although female critics do not review the work of women playwrights automatically more favourably, when it comes to work which has a feminist perspective, some male reviewers dismiss it out of hand. Sarah Daniels has perhaps most famously suffered in this respect. Inappropriately labelled as a 'man-hating playwright' and someone who is 'consumed with feminist anger', her play *Masterpieces* caused a major critical storm over a decade ago which she feels has still not entirely abated. It meant that her more recent play, *The Madness of Esme and Shaz* was approached with the same sort of distaste and negativity and that the critics couldn't objectively see what was in front of them or take on board her development as a writer. Lately an *Evening Standard* reviewer responded irrationally to April de Angelis's *The Positive Hour*, stating that 'De Angelis's dialogue frequently explodes into unwieldy, all-men-are-bastards diatribes' – discerning language which didn't even exist in her play. A critic shouldn't have to like a play or its politics for it to be good. As Carole Woddis noted in an interview with the *Independent*, 'Whose "good" and whose "bad" is it? I'm only one person.'

Sarah Kane also feels that there has been 'a failure by the critical establishment to develop an adequate language with which to discuss drama'. Her point becomes particularly important within the context of how ground-breaking work is reviewed. Phyllis Nagy believes that because critics are conditioned to watch only a certain kind of play, [of the exposition, crisis, resolution order] when they see something unfamiliar and they fail to understand it, they attack. Claire Armistead, arts editor of the *Guardian* agrees. She says that one of the biggest problems is that critics 'still take *Look Back in Anger*' [a play staged over forty years ago] 'as their benchmark. That's the aesthetic. We're still in the grip of the social-realists. That's how they see theatre,' she says. In a newspaper interview about the critical response, she admitted that, 'As a critic it's very intimidating when the work you are reviewing fundament-ally challenges the very precepts by which you write: linguistic, logical, linear narrative structures. That can lead to a defensive reaction which says, "This is not theatre." ' The issue clearly isn't specifically about gender. Michael Billington believes it's often to do with 'the literary training that critics undergo. There's still an Oxbridge, Eng. Lit. bias,' he says. But because women playwrights are predominantly challenging form, their work tends to suffer more at the hands of reviewers.

Claire Armistead draws attention to Caryl Churchill's plays, which although they are highly respected, have often been critically misunderstood. 'People are still saying to me, "Oh she doesn't understand structure" and I say, "absolutely on the contrary, she's reinvented structure." But they still haven't grasped it,' she says. On the matter of social-realism – which Michael Billington agrees is still regarded 'as the norm or the standard criteria by which plays are judged' – he does, however, acknowledge 'the difference women playwrights have made' by widening 'the definition of what is conventionally realistic – that exploration of fantasy, subconscious desires or dreams are as realistic as people sitting round a table'.

Billington resists the idea 'that critics are lagging behind the new female aesthetic. A play is a public event which has, on one acquaintance only to communicate something. It has to give you an impression of life. It has to give you a sustainable idea. And if it doesn't do that, the play isn't quite working.' But he admits that 'One hasn't always grappled with the best of women's writing as well as one should. With several plays that in retrospect have been landmark plays,' he says he has 'signally failed to rise to the occasion'. He cites Sarah Kane's *Blasted*, which 'I didn't get to grips with. I didn't like the play, but I deplore the tone with which I reviewed it, which was of lofty derision. I can now see that it was a serious play, driven by moral ferocity.'

Claire Dowie believes that a damaging prejudice is at play when it comes to the different way the work of male and female play-wrights is approached; that male critics judge the work of male playwrights hoping it will succeed, but that with women play-wrights it's often a case of 'let's see you fail'. It's a belief that Michael Billington strongly disagrees with. 'I don't think male critics think, "Oh goody, goody, David Hare. I know where I am. Phyllis Nagy, God knows what she's on about." One doesn't go in with that kind of attitude at all. You go to see a new play by any writer with a degree of optimism or curiosity.'

But there have been times when an inequality has been evident. Nick Ward's *The Present*, for example, which opened at the Bush at the same time as Phyllis Nagy's *The Strip* opened at the Royal

Court – both employing a non-linear structure – was approached comprehensively with a genuine desire to understand and make sense of its objectives. A *Daily Telegraph* critic wrote: 'I'm uneasily aware that the more I attempt to describe *The Present*, the more preposterous it sounds. But during the course of Ward's own mesmerising production, it all makes a kind of sense... *The Present* remains mysterious to the end. But there is no mistaking its atmospheric power, its sinister sexuality and its bracingly black comedy.' The same critic's review of Phyllis Nagy's play was not only headlined 'Completely Lost in Las Vegas', but described as 'too sprawling a piece for the stage... Nagy appears to be making it all up as she goes along, raising questions she has no intention of answering... There is a good deal less here than meets the eye. What seems intriguing is empty and pretentious.'

Vicky Featherstone believes that the negative expectation critics sometimes have of women playwrights is as much to do with their subject matter as their form. 'They expect something mediocre which isn't going to speak to them or concern itself with feelings that are of any interest to them, or any relevance to the things that they think are important in the world,' she says. 'And should anything remotely touch on what they see as "womany", they don't look any further. If it's about a mother and a daughter or best friends, that's it. They throw it out of the window. Regardless of the fact that the friends might have an incredibly complex relationship which also happens to be a metaphor for Eastern Europe and the space programme.' It's a point that Helen Edmundson also makes with regard to how her play *The Clearing* was reviewed.

'It's felt among critics,' says Claire Armistead, 'that women write in the private zone much more than the public zone. What they don't necessarily see is that the private can mirror the public. You don't need to make absolutely clear connections between the institutions of state and a state of mind in order for it to be political, public.'

Phyllis Nagy believes that this lack of perception about the quality of a lot of women's writing has also had an impact on the 'canonisation' of women playwrights. Critics don't tend to recognise women writers as 'great'. Charlotte Keatley draws attention to Michael Billington's recently published book of collected reviews *One Night Stands*, in which only two plays by a living woman playwright are included in the entire selection: Caryl Churchill's *Serious Money* and *Light Shining in Buckinghamshire*, [Nicholas Wright's *99 Plays* included five] falsely suggesting,

Keatley says, that theatre has been entirely constructed and created by men.

Clearly some changes need to happen if theatre criticism is to do justice to the wide variety of work which it surveys. Claire Armistead's progressive idea that the time may have come 'to challenge that notion of a critic as one person in a passionately knowledgeable position, pontificating' and instead to develop 'a polyphony of voices', would no doubt be welcomed by playwrights across the board, although she doubts it would be possible, 'unless on the internet because newspapers are so pressured for space'. Instead she suggests that, 'A different sort of rigour is needed' from critics. 'A rigour with one's own criteria for making judgement, as well as a rigour with the material you're offered.'

The future, however, looks bright for women playwrights. The next generation of critics (given that more deputies are female) looks set to be more balanced. Women are increasingly moving into key positions as literary managers, agents, producers, directors and artistic directors. Janet Paisley, Pam Gems and Yasmina Reza have recently won major awards (in the face of strong, male competition). The Women's Playhouse Trust have got the building they spent years fighting for, and development work at the National Theatre Studio is split equally this year between women and men. Most of the writers in this book are currently under commission to theatres. Many have gained international recognition for their work. Their plays are moving onto school and college syllabuses and 'There are astonishing women coming through', as Sharman Macdonald points out. But the best news, as these interviews evidence, is that we have such a talented and committed corps of women playwrights, who continue to craft outstandingly good plays. And despite their rage (maybe because of it), they have the reason and the spirit to carry on. The potential for theatre to be thrilling, even life-changing, is there.

Heidi Stephenson and Natasha Langridge,
June 1997.

Sarah Daniels

Brilliantly and savagely funny, Sarah Daniels's work has achieved major popular success whenever it has been produced, despite a seemingly endless barrage of vitriolic attacks from theatre critics. 'I feel ill-at-ease in her universe,' commented one *Times* reviewer, perhaps in response to the fact that Sarah Daniels does not shy from putting women very firmly centre-stage and attacking oppression with an anger and energy that is uniquely hers. The first woman playwright to have a full production at the National Theatre with *Neaptide*, in 1986, she was also the first to give the issues of lesbian women a prominent voice. Firmly grounded and positive in her approach and outlook, she creates empowering, vital and, above all, real women characters, who span the entire range and complexity of female experience, past and present. She may well be a threat to the establishment, but her audiences love her!

Sarah Daniels's plays include: *Ma's Flesh is Grass* (Crucible Studio Theatre, Sheffield, 1981); *Ripen Our Darkness* (Royal Court Theatre Upstairs, 1981); *The Devil's Gateway* (Royal Court Theatre Upstairs, 1983); *Masterpieces* (Royal Court Theatre Upstairs, 1983; Royal Exchange, Manchester, 1983; Royal Court Theatre Downstairs, 1984; and several productions in UK repertory and abroad, including in Germany, Japan, New Zealand and Australia); *Byrthrite* (Royal Court Theatre Upstairs, 1986); *The Gut Girls* (Albany Empire, London, 1988 and productions in New York and Denmark); *Beside Herself* (Women's Playhouse Trust, Royal Court Theatre Downstairs, 1990); *Head-Rot Holiday* (Clean Break Theatre Company, 1992); *The Madness of Esme and Shaz* (Royal Court Theatre Upstairs, 1994) and *Blow Your House Down* (The Live Theatre Company, Newcastle upon Tyne, 1995). Deservedly, but somewhat ironically, considering the amount of negative criticism she has received at the hands of reviewers, Sarah's work has also won several awards, including the George Devine Award for *Neaptide* in 1982, the London Theatre Critics' Award for Most Promising Playwright in 1983 and the *Drama Magazine* Award for Most Promising Playwright, also in 1983. She has written extensively for radio, where her work includes:

Purple Side Coasters (for BBC Radio 4), *Friends* (for BBC Radio 5) and *Annie On My Mind* (for BBC Radio 5). Her television work includes numerous episodes for the BBC television series *Grange Hill* and *EastEnders* and series 4 and 5 of *Medics* for Granada. Sarah's plays are published in two volumes by Methuen. A native Londoner, she continues to live south of the river.

*   *   *

You are celebrated as one of our best feminist dramatists. Is that what you set out to be?

I was a feminist when I started writing but I didn't start writing thinking, I'm going to be a feminist dramatist. I was going to write what I wanted to write. Having said that, when I wrote *Masterpieces* I did very much set out to write a play about violence against women and the issue of pornography from a feminist point of view. I think I felt that the approach of some feminists was rather academic (though of course that has its place) and that the issues weren't in a broad enough arena. I did write *Masterpieces* out of a genuine fury and passion.

Why do you think there have been so relatively few women dramatists? And do you think that women are given enough main-stage treatment?

I don't know that there have been so relatively few women dramatists, rather that they have often been forgotten, left out of the canon or remain unproduced. Aphra Behn's work, for example, was almost entirely ignored until the Women's Playhouse Trust did *The Lucky Chance* in, I think, 1984. There was quite an explosion in the mid-eighties, when paradoxically – and this is where feminism comes in – all sorts of opportunities seemed to open up. And I'm glad to say that there are more women writing and having their plays produced. Of course the more women dramatists there are, the more role models there are, so that it seems increasingly like an available option.

The answer to the second half of your question is simply, no. Of course there are women writers who deservedly have main-stage plays but not enough of them. The Royal National Theatre does have the word 'national' in the title – so where is half the population? I think theatres which receive public subsidy have an obligation to produce new work which reflects a cross-section of themes about different experiences in society. I don't think this view has anything to do with political correctness or positive discrimination, but fairness, and it shouldn't just extend to women but of course to black writers.

Yes, why does the Royal Court put playwrights like Winsome Pinnock Upstairs and not on the main stage? And why haven't you had a Downstairs commission, despite your track record?
I have, of course, had plays on Downstairs – *Masterpieces* which transferred from Manchester Royal Exchange and *Beside Herself* which was a co-production with the Women's Playhouse Trust, but I think that the Royal Court itself has never made the leap of faith with me.

Do you think mainstream theatres judge the work as too risky? Have you ever been asked to tone down the more radical elements?
At present it's surely all part of a wider context in which anything that isn't *Carousel* or attracts extra funding from private sponsorship is probably seen as risky, but I couldn't honestly say I'd ever been directly asked to alter things because they were too radical. That's not how it works. The pressures on managements, and so on everyone who works in the theatre, are very real but it all happens in a more subtle and insidious way.

Does it disturb you that feminism in the nineties is thought of as something passé?
I think it was always perceived like that from very early on by people who wished it would go away, but the fact remains that it has made a very big difference in all sorts of ways. But you have to remember that in its origin feminism had a very radical agenda to do with rights and justice and of course neither of those things have been too popular recently.

Do you think that one of the biggest problems feminist dramatists face is the fact that the vast majority of critics are still male?
Only if and when it blinkers their perception! Though it's not as simple as that. I have had some, although that might be overstating it, perceptive, fair and even flattering reviews from male critics and I've had a few snide reviews from women journalists. The thing was that *Masterpieces*, because it was so angry, seemed to create anger on the counter-attack which did ironically also stimulate interest in the play.

I think part of the problem for me (although I'll say this and then all the critics will change), is that the same critics are there, ever since I started writing. The same men who haven't forgiven *Masterpieces*. They have these positions, they have this power and

they have something in their heads about me, that however much
I change, deviate and move on as a writer, I'm not allowed to. In
their eyes I'm still exactly what they thought I was and I feel I'm
still getting a certain amount of punishment. This is difficult for
me to say, but with *Esme and Shaz*, for example, which was an
entirely different play, one which celebrated female solidarity and
resourcefulness, I felt the critics reviewed it with the same sort of
distaste and anger. They hadn't seen the play I'd written. I also feel
that the criticism has moved. They were much more open with
their anger and hysteria and defensiveness earlier on and now it's
more bland and damning which is much worse. I don't think I
have been, or necessarily ever will be, forgiven by a lot of them.

**Carole Woddis has described you as 'overtly political', someone
who has 'taken on issues that challenge some of the most sensitive areas of patriarchal society'. Is this how you see yourself?**
Some plays are more political than others, but within a context of
challenging a status quo and putting forward ideas or ideology that
have a different perspective, then my work is political. I do want
my plays to be challenging. A play, to me, should be relevant to
today's society; that's part of why I think you write plays. It should
tell a story and it should also challenge.

**What do you think about Benedict Nightingale's comment, with
reference to women playwrights and their work, that the best
plays transcend gender?**
What does that mean? What does it mean? It's just another way of
not facing things. The subtext of that is that the best plays are the
ones I like.

**You have come up against criticisms that you are a 'man-hating
playwright' and someone who is 'consumed with feminist anger'.
What do you feel about this?**
It's not about hating men, it's about putting the focus on women
and trying to say, 'Hey, look, this is going on. This is how it feels
from here. How can we redress it?' Feminism has put a different
perspective on a lot of human experience. Incest, for example, might
always have been a taboo subject, but there is a world of difference
between the sexual relationship of two consenting adults in the
same family and sexual acts done to a three-year-old by her father.
The latter now is no longer termed incest but sexual abuse. And
the change in perception came about not because some lexico-
grapher put another definition in the dictionary, but because women

started to speak up, often in the face of hostile criticism, disbelief and ridicule about their experience.

I have also been accused of being didactic. *Masterpieces* is an issue-based play and in that sense it is didactic. I don't necessarily think I would write like that anymore, but I don't feel apologetic for it. People said it was like a sledgehammer, but it was more like a scream really. If it had been more subtle, I don't think it would have had the impact that it did.

There is also this question of what else is happening. I mean it's been said that *Neaptide* is a play about depression, or in a more generalising way that the theme of depression is central to my work. Yet *Neaptide* was, in my mind, a play about lesbian custody and the fact of the matter is that these other climates filtered into it.

Yes, mental health issues seem to interest you a great deal. Why do you feel compelled to explore this subject in relation to women's issues?
If you write about anger you have to write about depression too, don't you? The two are somehow mixed up. I think powerlessness has a great deal to do with it. When women express anger outwardly they're often perceived as mad and dismissed as such – it prevents anyone having to take them seriously – like Mary, the mother in *Ripen Our Darkness* or Dee, Claudia and Ruth in *Head-Rot Holiday*. The other side of the coin is that it's then internalised and squashed and becomes depression. There's Evelyn in *Beside Herself* who is prevented from taking any worthwhile action by the voices in her head and having to deal with this abused lost child she takes round with her everywhere. Mental ill-health is a subject which does transcend gender, race, class and sexuality for that matter, but the social reasons for it more often than not don't.

Your plays are extremely funny and energising. Do you feel that humour is essential to radical drama?
I feel humour is essential to being human. Its uses are many and varied. It can be used to entertain or to challenge. I think if something makes you laugh you often remember it and it's thought now that people who laugh a lot live longer. Ridicule can often be a more devastating weapon than argument. And some things *are* ridiculous. When I wrote *Head-Rot Holiday* which I did for Clean Break, I met ten women who'd only recently been out of Broadmoor and interviewing them was really one of the most stimulating things I've ever done. The women I talked to had wonderful senses of humour and could laugh at the most *heinous* things. They

laughed at how ridiculous, how awful things were. You know the bit of Kate Millett in *The Loony Bin Trip* where she says you can be thrown in the same loony bin as your rapist? A large proportion of men in Broadmoor are in for repeated, gratuitous, sexually violent crimes and a very large proportion of the women in Broadmoor, whatever crimes they have committed, have been horrendously sexually abused as children, and they are encouraged to be 'normal', to go to the disco and dance with these men. It's horrendous, you know, the illogicality of it. But it's so horrendous it's funny – the idea that this is how to attain normality.

A *Daily Telegraph* critic made an absurd comment in his review of *Beside Herself*, saying, 'Sarah Daniels has not learnt to construct a scene, let alone a play,' and casting doubt on your right to have won the George Devine Award for *Neaptide*. Do you think it's something about women evolving new structures that critics just can't seem to handle?
There's two things here. Yes, I know that there are theories on evolving new structures but I believe that every writer strives for originality and the other side of it is that perhaps we don't demand enough of ourselves as playwrights in this respect. One of the things I feel is that style is often given more credence than content. I'm afraid I'm old-fashioned enough to think, 'I don't care how beautiful, ritzy, glitzy, dazzly or weird anything looks, I want to be intellectually and emotionally involved in it. I want to engage with it on a gut level.' Not all of us are genuine Picassos. I suppose I'm ducking the issue. For myself I feel that the criticism that I try and pack too much into a play is valid and this doesn't come from trying to evolve a new structure, but from lack of confidence in my ability to hold an audience's attention.

But playwrights like Caryl Churchill started off something that was non-linear and different, that moved away from one central character.
Yes. In that respect Caryl Churchill is Picasso.

Why do you think you are accused of using improbable scenarios and dialogue?
It's difficult to answer this without knowing which scenes and what dialogue it refers to. The easy answer would be that it is a way of undermining and dismissing the work out of hand. There are scenes in *Head-Rot Holiday*, for example, which were improbable because no one would want to believe that anyone in our society could be

treated like that, but they were based on factual accounts. And then there is the last scene in *The Madness of Esme and Shaz* which some people think is pure fantasy, but it's not intended that way. It's not so much 'And with one bound they were free' as that in a sense they have changed positions and that it's now Shaz who has to look after Esme – she's barely out of hospital herself and she's having to take on this geriatric nutter, so the ending is quite ambiguous, I think. They have both changed because of their love for each other and now it's Esme that needs help with her break-down, if you like. I didn't intend it to be happily ever after. They've still got an enormous amount of adjusting to do before getting anywhere near that point.

But the debate about improbability and unrealistic characters extends back a long way. Oscar Wilde said something like, and I'm probably paraphrasing wildly, (no pun intended) that the function of the artist is to invent, not to chronicle, and that the realism of life was always spoiling the nature of art, or something like that. Plays for the stage which rely mainly on dialogue to tell a story, unlike, say, novels or film, surely have licence for heightened language. Drama, for me, is the telling of a story where the unexpected (I don't mean melodramatic) happens. Where characters face dilemmas and make choices in situations that don't happen every day to everybody. Conversely, I often hear people say things that I could never put in a play because I think no one would believe it. I think some of the problem is that critics not only think that they know all about drama and theatre, but that they know all about the world, and they don't. People who talk about improbable dialogue don't really live in the real world.

There is clearly a need for more plays by women, but what else do you think is missing from today's theatre?
I think what's mainly missing now is new writing. The classics are done again and again, adaptations of novels are done, which is fine. I'm not saying that Ibsen or Shakespeare or novels should be kicked off the stage, but it should be in equal proportion. And I think there's too much emphasis on the new play having to be a success. When I first started writing people put plays on they believed in. Nobody talked about box-office. That's changed now because theatres have to consider how best to keep afloat, even subsidised theatres. But if they won't take risks, who will? It would be really interesting to see the statistics of new plays that go on and to see those broken down, because, of course, the National has a fairly high statistic because of David Hare, but if you took him and his

plays out, what would you be left with? I'm not for one minute saying that David Hare's plays shouldn't go on, but where are the new plays, the second and third plays by writers?

Your work has been predominantly directed by women. Do you find women more supportive to work with?
The most important thing is the relationship of the director to the play, that the director likes the play and wants to direct the play that's there and not some other play that's standing somewhere to one side of what I've written. When I was a lot younger it was a political decision to work only with women directors. I think I have been in print saying I would never have a man direct my work and I've since learnt to use the 'would never' more sparingly. It is rather a luxury now. There often isn't the choice and although it would perhaps serve the feminist argument to leave it there, it would be untruthful. John Burgess, who directed *Neaptide*, so understood the play that I was often delighted and startled at his insight and perception. And the other male director I've worked with is Teddy Kiendl who came to me with the idea for *The Gut Girls* and really helped me shape the play. So I have a relationship based on trust with both of them.

You've said that writing gets harder and not easier. Why is that?
In many ways it's comparatively easy to write a first play because you've got nothing to lose. It's quite exciting, in fact. And then it just seems to get harder and harder. It's partly the expectation you have of yourself and partly the perceived expectations you think other people have of you. You think, 'Oh I'm so much older now, I've written so much more, I should be cleverer than I am,' and that makes it harder. Some time ago I decided to let go of the criticism and the worry about people turning the play down and just to enjoy the writing. That made a big difference. But I still find it very difficult to start a play and I have a terrible tendency to rely on deadlines to force me into doing things. Weeks tick by and I find myself thinking I'll manage to draw some inspiration from morning television – which is a very big mistake, believe me.

Debbie Isitt

Refusing to submit herself to the confines of conventional theatre, where she felt she would do nothing but 'pick up bad habits and learn nothing', Debbie Isitt set up her own award-winning company Snarling Beasties (a Berkoffian term for 'testicles') in 1986, at the age of nineteen. Amongst the Beasties, she was able to explore and experiment outside the usual boundaries and to combine her talents as writer, director, actor and producer. Uncompromising, gutsy, sharp-sighted and seriously funny, she speaks with a rare and energising passion. Her commitment to theatre and her fierce belief in its power to effect change are absolute.

Debbie's work tackles social issues head-on, but is remarkable in its capacity to transform their exploration into fast, furious and highly entertaining theatre – going beyond Berkoff, to fuse emotional truth with heightened physicality. Her plays include: *Punch and Judy: The Real Story* (winner of *The Independent* Theatre Award 1989 and Perrier Pick of the Fringe; national tour and London West End season at the Donmar Warehouse; international tour, Australia and USA); *Femme Fatale* (*Time Out* Theatre Award 1991; Pick of the Fringe; national and international tour including Australia, South America, New Zealand and Spain); *The Woman Who Cooked Her Husband* (Perrier Pick of the Fringe, 1992; Royal Court Theatre; national and international tour); and *Matilda Liar!* (Royal Court Theatre and national tour, 1993). In 1995 the BT Biennial commissioned *Nasty Neighbours* which premiered in over a hundred amateur theatres across the UK. In 1996 Birmingham Repertory Theatre commissioned *Squealing Like a Pig* and the Belgrade Theatre, Coventry commissioned an adaptation of *101 Dalmatians*.

A lover of film because 'It is so damn sexy', Debbie's screenplays include *The Lodger* for Channel 4, *Femme Fatale, Queer Kings* and *Johnny Watkins Walks on Water* for Vincent Films. She recently directed *Dance for a Stranger* for Ipso Facto Films and a feature film of *The Woman Who Cooked Her Husband*, based on her play (for E/G/I Pictures in association with Vincent Films), which will be released in 1998. She is also a freelance theatre director. *The Woman Who Cooked Her Husband, Matilda Liar!* and *Nasty Neighbours* are published by Warner Chappell. Debbie has stayed true to her roots and lives in her home town, Coventry, with Beastie, her Great Dane.

* * *

You worked as an actress for the Cambridge Experimental Theatre Company for a year, before founding Snarling Beasties in 1986. What was it that made you get out of the conventional theatre and take control of your own work?
I trained at Coventry Centre for Performing Arts for two years and the second year was all about productions and practical experience. A lot of the work was very naturalistic and very male. I wasn't thinking in those days about male and female, but I understood that the parts for women were not usually as good as the parts for men. It was the very simple idea of a seventeen-year-old thinking, 'How come he's got all the best lines?'

When I left college I started doing the usual rounds of auditions and realised that apart from being up against hundreds of other young actresses for one or two parts, even when you got the job the parts would be shit and you'd be touring in some crap production of some crap play, in some crap part that you'd worked all year to get. It didn't take a lot of imagination to work out that I didn't want to do that. I wanted to work in a field that was going to be much more valuable to me in terms of self-fulfilment and artistic expression, so when the job came up with an experimental company it rang some bells. There was a really good mix of gender in that group and they were actively seeking women who were interested in putting themselves forward; who wanted to be slightly more active participants of the company. I got offered the job, took it and it was a really brilliant experience. It was very free and everybody had their own voice.

How did you come to set up Snarling Beasties?
Well, I'd spent eighteen months touring Europe with the Cambridge Experimental Theatre Company. We'd met a European audience and realised that they were interested in theatre that was dynamic and didn't necessarily speak their language, but spoke to them on a different level. That excited me. The idea that you could conceivably not understand the language, but could still read the emotions and enjoy the physical nature of the work. I was really burning to develop the ideas that I'd learnt from the Experimental Company and wanted to find a new way of making that work

accessible, because I recognised that it wasn't everybody's cup of tea, that there were huge gaps in audiences that liked experimental work and performance art and audiences that liked straight theatre. I thought there was, perhaps, an audience somewhere in the middle that was interested in accessible work, stories they could understand and that were perhaps even linear, but that weaved into that an exciting new style or form.

I didn't have a clue about how to proceed. I felt that devising was a possibility and somebody suggested I read a Berkoff. We hadn't studied Berkoff at college and I picked up *East*. I just thought it was absolutely fantastic. I still do think it's probably one of the best plays I've ever read in my life. It was so full of fury and spoke so eloquently about class and anger. It also had stage directions which encouraged you to move and I thought, 'My word, this could be something.' It was just luck that when I chose to produce *East* in 1986 and took it to Edinburgh that he was *numero uno* and people came! We were sold out. The fact that the work was then reviewed well too, meant that the next time we went back with a piece of my work, we got an audience. Bingo.

Has it ever proved difficult for you, or have you hit any barriers with directing and performing in your own work? How easy is it for you to switch hats?
I've hit lots of difficulties in terms of other people's perceptions of it being difficult. It's just what I do. It's much, much easier to combine them. It gets more difficult when you have to separate them. But people think of it as not only difficult, but an arrogant thing to do and particularly unbecoming of the female. The Arts Council refused to fund my work on that basis for years until it was demonstrated to them that, 'Ah, this might be working.' It was 1991 before I got an Arts Council grant. That was a lot of years to be doing a lot of national touring, which also had to be considered 'good' and 'successful' in Arts Council terms, before they would admit that it was okay to use a writer/director who also acted.

You have been heavily influenced by Steven Berkoff's charged, heightened and hugely physical theatre. Do you think you are naturally attracted to this form because it relies so much on the creativity and skill of the actor?
That's absolutely what it is. Having trained as an actor, I understand the actor to be the person who has that relationship between audience and play, and that without the actor's influence, correct interpretation, creativity, contribution, the dramatic experience

wouldn't exist. That's how the art form of theatre works. On that level I am influenced by his work, but I didn't see a Berkoff production until *Decadence*, so I resist the idea that I was influenced by his productions. When I did see *Decadence* I was quite disappointed with his slightly more superficial approach to acting. He didn't seem to mine the depths of the emotional work.

You take situations and emotions right to the edge, which results in extraordinary clarity and economy of expression. What do you do to achieve this?
When you listen to people who are expressing something that is important to them, they are very economical. People don't over-express when they want to communicate. They find a way and often it's action, not word, and sometimes it's very monosyllabic, but you get what they mean. I think I'm really conscious of being honest, of really trying to dig into what's behind everything. I'm conscious of peeling away layers of the human psyche and that process becomes a very personal thing as you sit in a character's body. You have to go through it and at the end of the day you come to the bottom and realise, 'This is it. This is me. I am a horrid, jealous creature with no morals. This is the base me.' Trying to find that with every character is the journey I go on as a writer, then as an actor, then as a director.

In *Punch and Judy* you re-examine one of the most entrenched stories that we are conditioned to accept as children, which like many others reinforces patriarchy and the bad treatment of women. You retell this story with several important differences, drawing attention to the issues of battery, harassment and mental cruelty, and you create a very significant and empowering ending for Judy and Judys everywhere. Does more of this type of deconstruction need to happen?
I don't know, really. It was just one of those strokes of, 'Of course! Punch meets Judy every Saturday morning on Brighton beach. Of course! I hated it when I was a child. Of course! this is a really good vehicle for exploring domestic violence, particularly if you're a physical actor.' That's it. I wouldn't profess to have sat down and thought about it the other way around – you know, 'Let me investigate archetypal . . . blah.' It just happened like that.

In the play you parody the male establishment – its solicitors, doctors, police and judges – suggesting a conspiracy. Is that why it was important to have Punch playing all those characters?

Yes. I think the idea of him being Everyman was important really. If you are being abused every man you meet becomes Him, potentially Him. From her point of view that's how it feels; that she is a pawn in a male conspiracy. It's very, very frightening. Once you really acknowledge the physical power men have over women, it can lead into quite a self-destructive path. But if we don't acknowledge that patriarchy is that powerful and that dangerous, then we can't fight it. We can't overturn it. We can't win.

Hilary's opening line in *The Woman Who Cooked Her Husband*, 'I first decided to cook my husband on the day he left me,' takes any surprise out of what is eventually going to happen to Kenneth and the suspense instead comes from discovering what leads up to this event. Why did you choose to structure the play like this?
It's funny isn't it, because I don't consider that I chose to do that. Again it just sort of happened. The play works via an emotional journey. What we are actually watching, what we are paying our money to see, is a woman's journey. Where we choose to meet that story doesn't really matter. It's not a 'whodunit'. It's about a woman who has been rejected, who has to find her way through at an age where she feels there's no future. I think it's been the most popular of my plays because it obviously speaks to a lot of people. When we did it in Australia the Ex-Wives Club came on the coach. They were all over fifty and all divorced women. They sat in the audience and I've never seen anything like the riot that happened that night. It was absolutely fantastic. They were crying and shouting and whooping. And afterwards they were all saying, 'This is my life! This is my life on the stage.'

There is absolutely no ambiguity in your writing of Kenneth. He is selfish, defensive, cowardly and ignorant. Did you get any negative feedback about his characterisation?
Interesting, isn't it? I met somebody only Saturday night who had read the play, a man, and he said, 'How did you write that role? Because it's me.' And I said, 'It didn't take much imagination really. I've lived amongst men.' And he said, 'That's exactly how I behave. I've been living with my girlfriend. I've just left my wife. Every little detail. How did you know?' I don't think he saw Kenneth as a negative character. I think he saw it as I saw it really – as being more sad than dastardly: an inadequate man, incapable of facing up to getting old in a way that Hilary is forced to face up to it. In the end Kenneth even kind of admits that. I think men

liked Kenneth because it said to them, 'Yes, we are weak and feeble, but we're funny aren't we? We will lose out and we know that, but that's the choice we make.' No man admitted to identifying with Punch. It was kind of, 'Yeah, I know men like that.' He's a cuddly kind of character really, old Ken. Tasty too!

By the end of the play, the two wives, Hilary and Laura, have almost literally buried their adversity and united triumphantly in their crime – the obstacle which drove them to hostility disposed of. Was it important that the women came together at the end and rightly turned their anger on Kenneth and not on each other?
Yes, of course. They recognised that it is very easy to put all your anger onto the other woman and to keep romantic ideals about the man. 'She threw herself at him', 'If it wasn't for her he'd still be with me', this is the thing you get over and over again. And for their sake, in order for them to get on with their own lives, they have to confront the real truth of the matter which is, 'He didn't want you, love. He's ditched you. Get over it and get on with your life. Don't make enemies out of your own sex when at the end of the day this is what it's about.' Traditionally we blame the other woman. It's just avoidance tactics. And that's why it's important that they come together and they recognise that in that moment. That without him they could so easily have been friends, like they were at the beginning of the play. What is it that stops them? Well it's that great, fat wanker isn't it?

In *Matilda Liar!* you show very explicitly the collusion that goes on within the nuclear family and the way each of the characters would fight to the death to hold on to the lies that protect them. Do you feel it is this fear of the truth and the refusal to confront it that lies at the heart of society's problems?
Yes. I know that at the time of researching *Matilda Liar!* – researching lies and truths – I thought I'd tapped into THE ONE. I thought, 'Oh, it's about gender. It's about power. No, no, it's this. This is IT. This is THE BIG ONE. This is what's at the core of everything!' It blew my mind. For ages I couldn't write anything because I was like, 'Jesus-emm-aghhh.'

No one really communicates directly or truthfully for fear.
For terror. And I had to look at what would happen if we did tell the truth. It's difficult, isn't it? Because when they do start telling the truth it all goes wrong. So you do feel as if it's not actually possible

to be brutally honest; that society couldn't function on that basis; that we do need lies as tools, but that we abuse them so that we confuse the issue and become a mess and get entangled in an emotional web. It's a really complicated thing. Once you're not in the habit of communicating honestly, not only with each other, but with yourself, then you find a new way of functioning, of putting up with, of accepting, of pretending and dreaming and fantasising. You find a new way of functioning in your life and when somebody turns round and says, 'But what do you really think?' You say, 'Well, it doesn't really matter what I think because I've found this new way of functioning and if I'm to now change my life on the basis of what I really think, then the last twenty years is blown out of the window.'

It's the same with friendships, marriages, families, everything. If we communicate, at every stage, honestly, keep questioning, 'Am I being honest with you? Am I being honest with myself?' then that's what makes healthy human relationships. But we as a society aren't taught how to do that. We aren't taught that that's important. Healthy communication is about asking questions, trying to find the answers and not fearing ridicule. If we followed this we would undoubtedly have a different society. And why, when there are lots of intelligent people in the world, aren't we getting together and introducing these kind of ideals? There must be a conspiracy against that. There must be other intelligent people who say, 'Well, we know all of that is possible, but we don't want that because we like it the way it is.' I was using the family to demonstrate that in society.

In *Matilda Liar!* it soon becomes clear, to the great disillusionment of Matilda, that even our fairy stories perpetuate lies, myths and fantasies that bear little resemblance to reality. Did you want to explore the power of myths and stories and how they affect our beliefs and expectations?
I was inspired by Belloc's 'Matilda' because as a child I heard the poem over and over again and I really loved it. Matilda who told lies and was burnt to death haunted my childhood and I really did fear that if I told a lie something bad would happen and that was reinforced by my Catholic upbringing. It was a big part of growing up for me, as were all those fairy stories and the idea of there being another place, another world, where things were safe and fine and happy. I believed in them. They are designed so that you believe in them. So it is a huge shock and disappointment when you realise, 'This is not how it's going to be.' You do build a Utopia for

yourself. Then slowly it starts to disappear and fade. You look and it's gone and you know it was never there. Jesus, what do you do with that? How equipped are you to deal with that? Because what is it that makes so many people mentally unstable, if not that?

That's why it was important for me that Matilda built her new Utopia. That she started to write. That she started to weave her own stories, tell new stories; stories based on information and truth and her own idea of what she could achieve. That was really important to me, that we don't just put up with the loss of these ideals, but that we reclaim them and start again and build new paths; become the scriptwriters of our own lives and sack the original writer.

Much of *Nasty Neighbours* is about how we, and the characters, misread and misinterpret other people and their actions, which starts off a prejudice and can culminate, as it does between Mr Peach and the Chapmans, in total war. What interested you about this exploration?

Well, I had read a lot and seen a lot of documentary material on neighbours at war. It struck me that here was another example of having lots of information on one level about something that seems to be plaguing our society and no *real* information about it. So we'd hear stories about a man going round to his neighbours because they wouldn't give him planning permission and blowing somebody's head off. We'd receive that information and think, 'God, he must have been a nutter, eh? I wonder what all that was about?' That's about as far as we tend to get. I just thought, 'I wonder what's behind that?'

Where that took me was that this generation of man – of working-class, middle-aged man who was promised the earth and who was promised that if he played by the rules he would be rewarded – has not been rewarded. He can't believe it. And who does he blame? That young middle-class twat who moved in next door, because he becomes every bank manager, everybody who ever promised him that he was going to be rewarded if he did the right thing. Suddenly Mr Chapman becomes Him and he has to destroy him or be destroyed. Peach is on the edge of a nervous breakdown because he's being conned and he knows it.

Your plays, as well as being hilariously funny and deeply tragic, contain a violence that matches Seneca's in its brutality – with Matilda cutting out her tongue with a pair of scissors perhaps

the most potent example of this. Why is violence so central to your work?
It's certainly not something that I ever think is going to happen. It's something about violence born of anger, violence born of despair, violence born of frustration. What interests me is the anger, despair and frustration. Violence is a natural product of that and it's a reality. It happens every day of the year. It's not something we can avoid. Men cook their wives. Jeffrey Dalmer cut their heads off and put them in the oven. People cut their tongues out. People cut off women's clitorises. It happens. I don't think I glamorise violence, but I do think we ought to look at it. It's there and I'm interested in why, and what it all means.

Your feminism comes through very strongly in all your work. Is part of your mission as a writer to create positive and empowering representations of women and to challenge the 'inevitability' of certain situations and behaviour?
What is more important to me than that is the truth, whatever that might be. If I discover that a character is a weak and feeble woman who loves being beaten up then I will write her that way. But it is my experience that that is not how women are. Simple as that. The feminism comes from the truth, not through any design of mine to be a feminist playwright, but simply from what I truly believe. And if that changes then the work will change with it.

You once said, 'I don't believe in being another person contributing to the mass. I want to make a difference, to advance the theatre.' How close do you think you have got to achieving your aim?
Not bloody far enough. And that's the truth. Oh God, how old was I then? I mean, I've known ever since I was a seventeen-year-old student that I was going to have a life in the theatre. I was able to say to myself, 'I'm a living, breathing, working artist. That's what I'm going to do all my life and I'm going to produce my own work so that nobody can stop me from doing that.' But I haven't done that career-hopping thing that I think you have to do to say, 'Yes, I have advanced the theatre.' I mean I do the work. I know there's an audience out there and I hope there will be new audiences and that the work will keep changing as I change and as I collaborate with other people.

It's very easy to allow this industry to silence you. You know, you can't get on in the right theatre, your play can't be put in the right theatre, you won't be seen. How do you overcome that? You have to reach an audience and that's the challenge for me, finding ways of widening an audience, getting the information to them; not because I want to be a famous theatre person, but because I want to help people's lives. That sounds really crass, but unless I felt like that I wouldn't do it. I do it because of the people that stand up afterwards and say, 'I feel empowered by that. Now I might be able to go and act on that.' In that sense I feel that I have much more in common with Brecht than with Berkoff. I believe in the power of theatre. I believe in the power of theatre to change people's lives and perceptions and so I need to get to the people and I'm aware that not everybody wants me to get to them, like they don't want lots of people to get to them, in this industry and beyond it. That's the challenge. How do you keep growing as an artist and yet keep fighting the system? It's a constant battle. I intend to stay with it.

Phyllis Nagy

A powerhouse of fury and wit, New Yorker Phyllis Nagy was heralded by the *Financial Times* as 'the finest playwright to have emerged in the nineties', when she came to live and work in Britain, following a two-week exchange with the organisation New Dramatists, which brought her to the Royal Court in late 1991. In her own words, she 'had a great time, fell in love and six months later came back here for good'. Why did she abandon American theatre? 'I think it was more a question of why did American theatre abandon me?' she says, with characteristic humour. 'Nothing was going on in America. Nothing at all.'

Recognising a unique talent, Stephen Daldry organised a co-production of *Weldon Rising* (December 1992) between the Royal Court and the Liverpool Playhouse, which launched her in the UK as a force to be reckoned with. Her completely original style of writing is hallmarked by her wonderfully idiosyncratic and imaginative characters (who range from female female impersonators, to travel agents who have never been anywhere and a baby in Ku Klux Klan uniform), and potent metaphoric imagery such as a melting city. Exploring the mysteries of interconnection and fate, she weaves the personal struggles and stories of her characters into a disturbing, but always entertaining, dreamlike landscape, which is at once engaging, funny, horrifying, mesmerising and profoundly affecting. Innovative and lateral in her approach, the action cuts backwards, forwards and sideways and celebrates the enduring hope of her protagonists in a world of brutality and dissatisfied frenzy.

Phyllis's other plays include: *Entering Queens* (Gay Sweatshop, 1993); *Butterfly Kiss* (Almeida Theatre, 1994); the multi-award-winning *Disappeared* (Leicester Haymarket, national tour and Royal Court Theatre, 1995); and *The Strip* (Royal Court Theatre Downstairs, 1995). Her plays *Disappeared* and *The Scarlet Letter* are published by Samuel French, *Trip's Cinch* by the Dramatic Publishing Company and Smith & Kraus, and *Weldon Rising* and *Disappeared* appear in a single volume published by Methuen. A collection of her work, NAGY PLAYS ONE, will be published by Methuen in

1998 and will include *Weldon Rising, The Strip, Butterfly Kiss* and *Disappeared*. Her play *Neverland* opens at the Royal Court Theatre in January 1998.

* * *

Your plays are all written in a unique, non-naturalistic style. Why do you choose to write like this?

I'm writing naturalism the way I know it. This is the way people speak and have conversations. They don't answer questions fully and speak in interior monologues to themselves – unless they're insane. It makes me angry when certain plays are held up as paragons of naturalistic writing, when they actually bear no relationship to any thought pattern or speech patterning I've ever encountered. I think I'm writing naturally and those people aren't. People are elliptical; we're associative. We never say what we mean, hardly ever. On the other hand, I could also say that because I choose to deal in heightened situations, often in compressed periods of time, that sort of style naturally emerges as a way to get across points succinctly and in a way that's pleasing to the ear.

It's very lateral, isn't it? Do you think women think that way more naturally than men?

More laterally. Although there are an awful lot of women playwrights who don't think like that who are also fine. They're just not anyone I'd rate. I think greatness depends in a large part on lateral thinking. Not just in playwriting, but in all the media. I can't think of a great novelist who isn't lateral, or a poet, or a composer.

Some critics have quibbled that your plays don't have a clear storyline and one referred to your 'continually leap-frogging plot'. How do you respond to that?

Actually those reviews puzzle *me*. I think my storylines, my plots, are crystal clear. The structure is crystal clear. Suzanne Moore had been to see *The Strip* and she said, 'It seemed to me it was about too much.' For God's sake. How could something be about too much? You complain when things aren't about anything, and there's certainly enough of that. Can't they pay attention to more than one thing at a time? (*She laughs, incredulous.*) They're not even being asked to watch two things at the same time. You just have to keep some information in your head. That's all. My lover's mother can tell me the plots to my plays, why can't they? It's because they're conditioned to watch a certain kind of play, night after night after night. I think it dissolves the mind. I really do. So partly it's not their fault. They're so insecure when they can't say a thing about the play, because they haven't understood it, so the only thing they can do is attack. They do it to everyone.

It's interesting because there was a critical comparison going on at the time of *The Strip* with a play by Nick Ward called *The Present*, which opened at the Bush at the same time. And all the reviews for *The Present* were about how weird and unfathomable this play was, 'But isn't it brilliant?' And for me? The opposite.

But it's easy to understand why a lot of really first-rate, challenging women's drama completely bemuses some male critics because when women dramatists are at their best they tend to be structurally beyond any male dramatist. The mind at work is operating very differently. It's an open-ended examination of form that carries on throughout the finite piece of work. Men, even the really good ones, write thesis plays, no matter what kind of play they ultimately think they're writing. 'I'm writing a play about Bosnia,' or 'I'm writing a play about this and I believe this thing exists and my play is proof of that.' Whereas I think women say, 'I have an interest in this, but I'm not sure if these questions can be answered.' That's the difference. So a male critic confronted with both that kind of boldness structurally and an open-ended questioning, constant enquiry . . . Men have a need for closure and anal-retentive methods of reaching conclusions. Women don't; although it doesn't mean that the work is any less rigorous or patterned or structured. It's rare enough to see a play that is really and truly excellent. The critics don't see them. Six nights a week they see some crap like . . . I don't want to name names, but I just don't think that the standard of criticism is such at the moment that people can tell the difference. And because bad plays get good reviews, that's the standard against which, conversely, very good work is judged. So Edward Bond is always going to lose. Caryl Churchill's always going to lose. *The Skriker*, a very great play, is not given a first-rate production. Which critics spotted that? If that had been David Hare, Richard Eyre would have taken some responsibility for it. What is going on here? And it is the women's work that suffers that way.

You watched a lot of films when you were younger. Do you think this has influenced your style of writing? One critic saw a road movie in *The Strip*, for example.
Yeah. That's interesting. Because actually, yes, watching a lot of movies taught me how *not* to write a play. I'm not saying this to blow my own horn, but I can't think of a play with a more perfect

theatrical structure than *The Strip*. It's not cinematic structure at all. But again, few critics know the difference between televisual structure, film structure and sheer theatrical structure. You would have thought that living in this country with Shakespeare for hundreds of years would have taught them something about theatrical structure. Most critics don't recognise the predecessors to this play, which is incredible. It's not new. All the best ancient drama did things that way. But apparently, you can't do it anymore. After I finished *The Strip*, I thought, I'm not quite sure how I did this, but I'll never write anything like this again. Not quite like this. For me, it's a perfect play, structurally. It's not just emotionally or intellectually compelling, it's both of them together.

You always listen to music when you write. Music also plays an important part in your plays and you are very specific about its use. What sort of influence does it have?
Well, I think the major influence is a structural influence. I actually think that plays are structured the way certain forms of music are structured. It's been terribly important. It's been the single, greatest influence. I actually couldn't write anything without bearing in mind the principles of musical composition.

You have said that you write your plays in one six-day sitting and spend 359 days of the year thinking about the new play. What gets you to the point where you're ready to write? And what preparation do you make for this one, vital sitting?
I don't know. (*She laughs.*) I mean, now that I'm getting older, it's more like eight days. It'll grow to ten days soon, I feel. I don't know what gets me to that point. I have no idea. It is always the same, and before I do get to the actual writing period, I'm like some kind of cat predicting an earthquake. It drives everybody I know insane. I can't sit still. I'm bombarding myself. And usually I know it's going to happen when I start renting five or six videos a day and just watch them continuously. Somehow there's some mechanism that says, 'Okay. You've reached saturation point with the information you've gathered.' It's not even as if I do research. It's that everything I've taken in over that year somehow finds its way into the play. Not literally, but in a lateral way, that gives them a living edge.

Do you know what you're going to write when you get to that point?
Well, yeah. It's like carrying the entire play in your head, structur-

ally, and specifically the opening section and the closing sections. In between just occurs right there and then.

Does it pour out?
I suppose if you can call ten to twelve pages a day 'pouring out', but not really. It's more careful than that. I can never believe writers who say, 'The character just took over. Suddenly it was writing itself.' Are you crazy? You are crazy. I mean, that doesn't happen except with schizophrenics, you know. I think I understand what they mean, but you are ultimately completely aware. It's your vision and your voice and what you would like to get across that's coming through each of those characters. You're completely conscious of everything you're saying and doing. You manipulate them. That's the other thing, when playwrights are accused of manipulation by critics, you think, 'Well, excuse me, but that's exactly what it is.' It isn't like some mystical process whereby no one knows what they're doing and the writer sits there and waits for the ghost of Rudolph Valentino or whatever. We're not mediums. And yet there are writers, acclaimed writers, who are very bad at perpetuating that myth. You know, the dialogue medium. I *wish* there was a dialogue medium because then I could write plays in two days.

Do you make many revisions after that?
No.

So that's it. No first, second, third drafts?
It's a bit of a fib. Some people spew things out on the page just to get it out. I'm not like that. There are writers like that who do go through many drafts of things. I'm not one of them. I write what I mean to write immediately and it very rarely changes. I think the biggest rewrite, which I would consider to be a conventional rewrite, would have been *Weldon Rising* in which I veered away from my usual method of writing plays and just made a deliberate decision to write the play right now, and as a result it wasn't right. But that's it. *The Strip* was as is, with the exception of the scene in the bar between Martin and Lester. That scene was slightly resculpted and that was it. *Butterfly Kiss* had two lines rewritten.

I don't do script meetings. I don't tell you what the story is in advance. We agree on a subject, I vaguely tell you what I might do and then leave me alone and I'll give you the script. It's amazing how many people will agree to this. Not enough writers try it on. I've seen writers, really good writers, go through hell delivering a script to a theatre and then the theatre fucks them about for eighteen months. It happens with women a lot more than it happens with men, and for better or worse, I will not submit to that.

You describe your plays as 'comedies' and your work is very funny, if, at times, disturbingly so. Why is this so important to you?
I don't know if it is. They just are. You know, I think to myself 'That's perfectly ordinary behaviour. I know people who behave like that the whole time. Is that weird?' Also, very seriously, if you can make people laugh, they will listen to almost anything you have to say. So, *Butterfly Kiss* got away with itself because it was very funny. Yes, you lose some people that way, some very horrified people who think 'This is no laughing matter.' But those people aren't worth having. And the critics are clearly horrified sometimes by that kind of thing. I think, 'Well if you think Joe Orton's so fucking funny, why don't you think this is funny?'

'Female impersonation is rather a curious career choice for a woman, Miss Coo,' is the hilarious and serious opening line of *The Strip*. Is Ava Coo the representation of what a lot of women have become, caricatures of what they are supposed to be?
Yeah. That's the short answer. Women clearly have been reduced to becoming impersonations of themselves in order to get anywhere. Look at the sort of role models that are being held up. Madonna is a female impersonator, has absolutely become one before our eyes. And it's quite brilliant and also horrifying. Women like Camille Paglia are female impersonators as well, but different. So, yes, Ava is my commentary on modern womanhood gone berserk.

Suffocating and deluded mothers people your plays, especially in *Butterfly Kiss*. Do you want to bring the love–hate relationship between mothers and daughters out into the open? Remove the taboo?
I'm so tired of seeing mother–daughter plays where they're all so nice to each other. But you can't win because for every step forward a female dramatist takes writing a mother–daughter play that is actually honest, or tries to grapple with the issue, you get ten of those (the dishonest plays) shoved back in your face, with critical approval too. The way that Ava Coo and Tina Coo behave and the way that Jenny and Lily Ross behave – and *Entering Queens* has another quite deranged mother-and-daughter relationship – I mean,

I see it. I see it in my mother. I see it in friends' relationships with their mothers. Every time I come across this sort of, 'Oh darling, let me help you,' I mean, where do they come from? What secret are they harbouring? To me that's the alien. I think women want those relationships explored. Men don't want them explored. Because it would deny the primacy of the father–son relationship and the mother–son relationship, which is a great, male wet-dream.

You have been attacked by the gay press for creating unsym-pathetic gay characters and for appealing to male voyeuristic fantasies when you chose to show Tilly and Jaye's love-making in _Weldon Rising_. Do you feel under pressure from this censorship?
It used to upset me a lot more, because I think, actually, that my plays are more intensely gay-sympathetic and flag-waving even than anything by Jonathan Harvey. I don't understand it. I'm at a loss. All I can say is that I do know that the more complex a portrayal of a character, the less likely they are to acknowledge that it's positive. Because in portraying complex characters people aren't nice. People have their foibles, and it is what ultimately makes audiences come round to your point of view. If you write a play in which all the gay characters are so good you can't quite believe it, then my mother's going to walk out of the theatre. Fine, if you show her something she's likely to do herself or behaviour she has engaged in herself, like we all lie and we all cheat and we all from time to time do lots of bad things, she's more likely to go along with it. It's not healthy to deny that there's no division within oneself, let alone in the entire gay community. And what could be more positive and celebratory than the final ten minutes of that play?

Alienation also seems to be an important concern for you. Do you see Marcel, who 'is the third person' as the embodiment of modern society?
Yes, Marcel! He is what many of us are becoming. He's less than the sum of his parts. That's exactly what's happening to everybody, not only alienation on that personal level, but in relationship to one's own society. There's no correlation between what Marcel sees himself as and what the rest of the world will see. And there's no attempt to even bridge that gap, or to understand that the gap exists. The issues of personal responsibility and courage are also important. The situation is getting worse, specifically in the gay community, but in society at large, the faster we approach natural saturation points. The planet's being used up. Goodwill is being

used up. Everything is being used up. And the more insular we become, the less likely we are to accept responsibility for anything, including our own minds. My fear is that either what happens to the characters in *Weldon Rising* will happen to everyone eventually, or something much worse than that will happen. It's an insidious moral decision, rather than an unconscious decision, not to participate, not to help anybody, ever.

Three of your plays, *Weldon Rising*, *Butterfly Kiss* and *Disappeared*, feature a murder or hint at one. Is it that you want to examine the relationship between societal and personal breakdown?
I'm completely fascinated, always have been, by the nature of violence and what separates those of us who can commit violent actions from those of us who can't. Also, there's a correlation between violence and personal responsibility and lack of responsibility towards society and alienation. It's about identity and loss of identity. It's a natural extension of all my themes, carried to the nth degree. Mostly it's violence that's perpetrated within the family unit or certain sorts of personally directed violence. So in *Weldon Rising* I wasn't so much interested in the act as in the response to the act. *Butterfly Kiss* is also to do with response to the act, but the act itself as well, is a great taboo. But there's no shock value in seeing the act. I'm not interested in staging atrocity. The plays are very visceral and emotionally fuelled, but they also have an intellectual component which is quite conscious and which demands a certain objectivity from an audience.

You seem very interested in psychic phenomena and the whole question of fate. Certainly your characters either believe in it or are affected by it. And everything is connected in *The Strip*. Do you personally believe there is sense out there? Or are you exploring nineties society's obsession with finding some sense?
Well I think both. I'd be lying if I didn't say I believed in it myself, because there are too many, I was going to say, acts of coincidence that have occurred in my own life. But then I think there are no coincidences. That's the other tension that fuels both my work and my personal life. I think things happen for a reason. I'm not sure I know what those reasons are, as Tina Coo says, but I know that there is a reason, and without that reason there is a lack of hope. I think you've got to believe that there's a plan, or maybe not and it's just comforting to believe it. I think within that plan, though, the trickiness is taking responsibility. Because it would be very

tempting to believe that no matter what, we're fated to win the Olympic gold medal, or we're going down in the TWA crash, and it doesn't matter what you do. But I think it does matter greatly what you do, and what we do has an effect on the plan. The work tries to explore that angle always. Do the choices we make affect how our lives might be different?

You've gone on the record saying 'most of the plays I admire are not by women. That whole "wombic" element in women's writing really pushes my buttons.' What did you mean by this? What I think is that for too long women's plays, or the women's plays that were allowed to be produced, were all about the process of being a woman, as filtered through the eyes of men. So if there were plays about caring mothers or pregnant women or women's relationships which conformed to these male artistic directors' notions of what we all should be interested in, those plays got on. And as a result, that's mostly all we saw. Even in the late seventies, when plays of protest by women started seeing the light of day, they were still about the same thing, very narrow, domesticated. And I thought, 'This really is insidious,' because not only is it the only thing that's encouraged, but because it's the only thing that's encouraged women are writing it. And where is the work by women that addresses the big, broad issues of our time? Well, they're there, certainly. Caryl Churchill has always tried to address the big issues, but it's much harder for that work, when it's written by women, to get on.

But similarly, it's been my experience whenever a women's theatre company has asked me to meet them, it's symptomatic of the whole society, but invariably they'll say, 'We want this to reflect the experiences of all women.' And you think, 'Well what does that mean?' What does that mean? All the women I know don't have children. I know one woman who's had a baby recently. In my experience, no woman I know sits around talking about how hard it is to live without a man.

But if we're talking 'great' playwrights, I think there are as many great female writers as there are male. I mean, who's a great playwright? A great male playwright working in England? There's Bond, and Brenton, he's terrific. I can say Chris Hannan is going to be. Martin Crimp has written some great plays. But the people who are thought to be great: Tom Stoppard, Peter Schaffer ... I mean, all these people. What about Caryl Churchill? She is clearly a great playwright and Timberlake [Wertenbaker] has written big plays. Sarah Kane has the potential to be great and Marina Carr certainly has, on the evidence of *Portia Coughlan*. And people from the past who haven't been credited as great: Susan Glaspell is a far better playwright than O'Neill. Sophie Treadwell has written some very important and influential plays, but when they're performed they're always treated as museum pieces, very condescendingly. We never get to hear about the great plays by women. The critics don't recognise women as 'great'. I don't know if they even regard Caryl as great, but I bet you they'd put Pinter on the list. And when did he last write a great play? Timberlake is a far more insightful social observer than say, David Hare. And then men who really do write like women, like Howard Barker, he has a very lateral mind, he's written some very important plays, but he's unfairly vilified by the press, for, God forbid, using his brain. But men get more opportunities. They get staged. They get coverage. And if things carry on the way they are currently, with this 'laddism', this ridiculous promotion of men and bad plays and misogyny, then I, for one, will stop writing plays. I will no longer be a playwright in that sort of theatre culture. I will find something else to do instead.

Anna Reynolds

Drawing on the darkness, pain and truth of her experience in prison and psychiatric hospital, where she served a sentence for matricide before being released on appeal, Anna Reynolds channelled her indomitable energies into realising herself as a talented and engaging playwright. Her first play, *Jordan* written in collaboration with actress-writer, Moira Buffini and, based on the true story of a woman who killed her baby and the tragic circumstances which led up to that, premiered at the Lilian Baylis Theatre, London in 1992, won the Writers' Guild Best Fringe Play Award and heralded her as a major new voice in the theatre. With humour and dignity, she journeyed determinedly through the notoriety of her past and the media circus attached to it, to create plays which have a raw power and a profound and compassionate understanding of the human condition. Her work offers a rare insight into life on the inside, the brutality of the judicial and penal systems and the complex motivations of human beings who have been driven to the edge. Deeply moving, brave and provocative, she confronts reality head-on, prioritising the individual, not the issue, and without ever making a sentimental plea for sympathy, leaves us to judge for ourselves.

Her other plays include: *Wild Things* (for Paines Plough, Salisbury Playhouse and national tour, 1993); *Red* (for Clean Break Theatre Company, which opened at the New End Theatre in 1994, before touring to prisons); and *Precious* (which opened at the West Yorkshire Playhouse in June 1997). Her television work includes *Paradise* (a First Film Foundation, Diverse and BBC 2 co-production). She has also written a novel, *Insanity* (published by Fourth Estate), and an autobiography, *Tightrope* (which was withdrawn from publication by the Home Office). Anna is currently Writer-in-Residence at the University of Essex/Mercury Theatre, Colchester and is working on a screenplay, *Ride*.

* * *

What made you start writing for the theatre?
It was an accident. A friend of mine was an actress and she wanted

to get some interesting work in the theatre, so I wrote a play and she performed it. I'd never thought about writing for the theatre before because I'd never been to the theatre, so I didn't know anything about it, which was probably a good thing at the time because I wasn't thinking, 'Oh God, this isn't what a play should be.' We put it on ourselves and when I saw what you could do I just thought, 'Wow!' I had this incredible high.

Were you surprised by the media coverage that was generated when your first three plays were produced?
No. It was one of those horrible inevitabilities really. It was just too irresistible to people. And if you don't do the interviews they'll write about you anyway, so at least you can kid yourself you have some degree of control if you actually talk to these people.

Jordan **examined infanticide in a new and much more sympathetic way than it had perhaps ever been looked at before, where Shirley's suffocating of Jordan is not a psychopathic act, but one of desperation and mercy. Why was this important to you?**
Because it was a true story. I was in gaol with her. The story of the real Shirley is pretty horrific and it really affected me. I wanted people to hear it because nobody really cared. If someone hangs themselves in gaol it's not a big deal. It's just like, 'Oh, another one.' And I thought, 'This is not the right way to treat these things. We should realise that they've got a bigger meaning for society.' But one thing I always try very hard to avoid is making the characters victims, male or female, because I don't find that dramatically interesting. The women I write about might not have much self-esteem and they might think they're crap, but they'll think it in a stroppy way, 'Yeah, I'm crap. So what?' One of the things I liked about Shirley was that she was saying, 'Some of it's my fault and some of it's not.' I always thought she was quite strong-minded in a way: 'I'm gonna die. That's my choice, so fuck off, leave me alone and get out of here.' There's a horrible inevitability about knowing that things aren't going to change. She was on a rollercoaster and she couldn't stop it happening. And things in society have gone too far for us to say, 'Put a plaster on it and everything will be all right.'

Do you feel compelled to force society and audiences to confront the reality of life on the inside and the hell that inmates go through?
Certainly with *Wild Things* I desperately wanted to write about

the situation you are put in when you are thought to have some sort of mental illness. I'd always been very angry about that and I'd never known how to deal with it. It's quite difficult to be angry about prison in a sense, because prison doesn't pretend to be anything else. I've talked to people who've been in gaol and though they might have had horrific experiences, the thing they were still having nightmares about twenty years on was some sort of hospital experience. You assume that you're in a safe place when you enter a hospital of any sort and then you realise very quickly that you're in the most dangerous place you could be.

Psychiatrists and their totally inappropriate methods of sedation and assessment come under angry attack in all your plays. Can you tell us a little bit more about this?
If I do have villains they probably are shrinks. I tried to tackle that in *Wild Things* because I did feel that Dr Trick was trying to be a force for good. She was just working within a system that didn't allow her to have any leeway. Psychiatry has very rigid limits that don't allow people, doctors or clients, to be individuals. The whole practice looks at people as if they are dangerous animals that need to be contained in some way, as if all you can do for them is to give them some sort of medication. I'm sure in some hospitals they do give proper counselling, but rarely. In most places, they just stick needles in people. We have all these different forms of helping and treating people and yet we stick to that because it's easier and cheaper to have a psychiatrist behind a desk making a rapid assessment of somebody and labelling them with a mental illness. And then it's tempting to just be crazy because somebody has told you that you are anyway.

The law sees everything in black and white and won't allow for complexity, explanation or anger, particularly where women are concerned. Do you feel very strongly about this? Certainly Kay does in *Red*, which comes up most potently when she satirises the justice system in her mock trial of Gerda.
I got a lot of flak from a couple of radical feminist organisations who said, 'You should be portraying these women as the victims they are and not as women who are prepared to use and abuse the system.' For God's sake, women have to protect themselves in court. It's survival. Come on, you know. I didn't want to write something that said, 'These women are victims of a male system.' I wanted to say, 'This is these women's story. Make up your mind for yourself.' There were two women who were in that position

who really interested me. One was very, very timid and very frightened all the way through the appeal process. She was seen as the
victim and the public empathised with her. And then there was
Sara Thornton who probably says things she shouldn't say and
wears clothes she shouldn't wear, but she is herself. She could easily
have assumed an image, done what the lawyers told her to do and
it would have been a damned sight easier getting her out of gaol.
Women are treated in a certain way by the legal system, in a way
that men aren't. Men are treated more on the basis of what they
have done, rather than on what everything around them adds up to.

The only way that Kay, a fairly street-smart woman, could get
to a position of truth would be to play the system in the way that
the system was playing her. There are no grey areas. You can't say,
'I know it looks like this, but if you understood how I was feeling,'
because the fact is that when Kay finally kills David she's actually,
in a sense, got no reason to kill him. She's been through years
of mental abuse, but she can't say, 'Look, I had eleven years of
somebody destroying my life.' She has to say, 'He threatened me
with a knife, so I put one on him,' which is the realisation Kay
gets to. Gerda is thinking about what is morally right, what she
can live with. Kay is thinking, 'I have to get out of here.'

**In *Red*, Dr Trick talks to Johnny about his future 'out there'
and Johnny replies, 'This is there. This is part of the world.' Do
you feel it's time society took responsibility for its problems
instead of locking people away?**
Yes, but by having people like Johnny out in the community with
no real care or anything spent on them, it's almost like the Government is saying, 'Well look, we're taking care of you. We're not
locking you away in the old asylums.' It's a lot cheaper. They want
to sell off buildings. They can make staff redundant and it saves
money, but in the long run, of course, it doesn't because people
like Johnny can't cope. They end up having to go back and there
are no beds for them. It's chaos. And Diane in *Red* is partly based
on a woman who'd been in a hospital for twelve or thirteen years,
originally because of shoplifting. It was one of those things that
had just escalated horribly.

***Red* toured to prisons after its run at the New End Theatre and
you took part in post-show workshops with inmates. Was this
an important experience for you and do you think inmates
benefit from seeing this sort of theatre?**
It was a very odd experience for me because I didn't believe, and

I'm still not really sure that I do, in taking theatre about prisons into prisons. It's a bit like having your nose rubbed in it over and over again. And the prisoners weren't really given a choice. It was, 'Either you're going to be banged up all afternoon or you can come and see this play.' So they all came. I don't know what they were expecting. They hadn't been told anything about it and I did feel at one point, 'This is not a good thing to have done. These people are mostly lifers. They're watching two lifers. It's not got a happy ending for Christ's sake and there are no songs in it.' What worried me was that people would come and see it, but if anything upset them or touched a nerve, they wouldn't have any way afterwards of dealing with that. They would just have to go back to their cells.

In some of the gaols it was okay. We went to a couple where there was a much more relaxed atmosphere. They were allowed to sit around with us for a couple of hours afterwards and talk. And because there were a lot of ex-prisoners involved with the play, they were saying, 'Oh God, you've done it. You've got out and done it. Good for you.' They loved that. Not only the fact that you could get out, but that you could make something like this, make theatre. And they were the ones who screamed, shouted and whistled Kay on. They kept ad-libbing her lines for her!

All your stage plays so far have examined the world of the secure wing or the psychiatric ward. Do you plan to write about other situations or is this territory that you still have things to say about?
I have just written a new play which is about none of those things. I did want to move away from all that, partly because I kept getting accused of trading on my experiences, 'And wasn't it all getting a bit dull?' After *Red* I just thought, 'No. I can bring these themes in without having to be so aligned to it all.' It was like I was some sort of representative. People would ask me, 'What do you think about the plight of prison?' and I'd say, 'I don't know. I haven't been there for years.' But then it's incredibly rare for someone to come out of gaol and write plays about it.

You've said that eventually you'd like to set up your own production company to encourage new writers. Do you feel that not enough new work, particularly by women, gets produced?
We've got more new plays than ever, but at the expense of actually giving people the time to develop. It seems now that you have your first play on and if it's a hit then great, but you've got to come up with another one very quickly. If you don't, or your second play

is not as good or is different, or doesn't come for three years, then
you can forget it. You have to get a new job or go into television.
So what happens to the stage? What happens to the theatre? And,
of course, the boys make more noise because of the things they're
writing about – macho Kalishnikovs and stuff. Most theatre managements, it seems, don't want to get back to what really matters.
They don't want to see plays about 'new men'. They don't want
to see plays about guys being understanding or being thirty-some-
thing. It's escapism. Whereas women are still steadily examining
the human condition in quite a profound way and are . . . where?
You don't get to hear about their work in the same way. I'm
concerned about the inequality of interest. I'll never forget seeing
Judith Johnson's play *Uganda*. I couldn't believe it. Nobody seemed
to be really excited about it and I thought, 'Why isn't everybody
all over the place about this? This is what we need.' And Gill
Adams, when she had *Off Out* on. That was not a 'female play'.
That was a hard, in-yer-face and up-yer-arse play and they had to
cut performances because they didn't get the audiences, yet it had
brilliant reviews.

Everything is dominated by marketing now. If you can't get the
headlines who's going to get excited about your work? What can
they pin it to? What can they write articles about? And boys are
running buildings and they're mostly hiring boys to write plays
about boys. I went to a theatre a couple of years ago to talk about
a commission and the guy said, 'What do you want to write
about?' I said, 'I want to write about these two gay guys,' and he
said, 'Why don't you write about an armed robber?' because I'd
just told him a story about my partner at the time who was an
armed robber, and he was getting really excited about this. It's the
whole Tarantino culture, isn't it? Which women either avoid (which
means they don't get bums on seats), or have to ape in some way,
or try to subvert, in order to have any success. It seems as though
Hollywood has invaded the theatre and this whole obsession is
actually filtering down into subsidised theatre! Theatre and film
are entirely different and they should be different. Surely the whole
point of the theatre is that, like Beckett, you can just have one or
two people hardly doing anything and it can be the most shocking
thing you've ever seen because of what's been said and what hasn't
been said. All those intricate things. I think that's why our twenty-
two to twenty-three-year-old playwrights move so easily now
between the two media, because they are becoming one. Theatre
can be so subtle and amazing. I want to be in a different place
where things are quieter and far more scary in many ways. If

theatre has gone past that, then I don't see much point in doing what I do.

Maybe the answer is to start up a production company. Every time I've worked with other women, and it's not accidental at all, I've had a bloody great time. I'm not prepared to write to prescription and I don't want to be pigeon-holed. And if I'm going to work in theatre, I want to be able to do the absolute business with it. If I just needed work I'd go to television. That's where a lot of playwrights are headed now. A lot of people in the last five or six years have thought, 'Well, I've put my heart and soul into this and you've ignored it or you've trashed it, so I'm off to write some episodes for telly.' It's a crying shame and something's got to be done about it.

Helen Edmundson

Helen Edmundson was born in Liverpool in 1964 and grew up on the Wirral and in Chester. She studied drama at Manchester University and worked extensively as an actress, director and deviser, most notably with the women's agitprop company Red Stockings, for whom she wrote her first solo piece, *Ladies in the Lift*, in 1988 and through which her talent as a playwright was first discovered. On leaving the company she continued to work as an actress before her second play, *Flying*, was presented at the Royal National Theatre Studio in 1990. This was followed by *The Clearing*, a passionate and poetic exploration of cowardice and conviction set in a seventeenth-century Ireland overrun by Cromwellian invaders. The play, which was first performed at the Bush Theatre in 1993, was joint winner of the John Whiting Award and marked her out as a playwright to be watched.

Helen is perhaps best known and widely celebrated for her ingenious stage adaptations for Shared Experience, where her capacity to transform mammoth and complex literary classics into vital, living theatre is nothing short of awe-inspiring. Rooted in a strong theatricality, her works, to date, have captured the essence of Leo Tolstoy's and George Eliot's artistic visions with precision, power and energy, successfully weaving physical expression with the spoken word to create sensual, richly distilled stage imagery.

Inventive and original, her adaptations stand alone as unique works and include: the multi-award-winning *Anna Karenina* (Tricycle Theatre and national tour, 1992); *The Mill on the Floss* (Lyric, Hammersmith, 1994) and *War and Peace*, which premiered at the Royal National Theatre's Cottesloe to great acclaim in 1996. Her television work includes two short films, *One Day* (BBC2, 1991), and *Stella* (Channel 4, 1992). A film version of *The Clearing* is currently in development. *Anna Karenina*, *The Mill on the Floss*, *War and Peace* and *The Clearing* are published by Nick Hern Books.

* * *

You worked first as an actress before turning to playwriting. Do you think your knowledge and experience of performance have given you the necessary theatrical vocabulary, the devices and tricks to adapt and write?

It definitely helps. If I'd just been a straight actress it might not have helped so much, but because I had my own company and we were doing agitprop and it was very basic theatre using lots of comedy and songs, I think we got a very good sense of how an audience works. We were constantly doing live shows to very different kinds of audiences and we got terrible responses and fantastic responses. It really helped me get a sense of how to draw an audience in, how to get them emotionally engaged, when to hit them with something completely different and how to turn the tables.

It also helps in terms of writing lines for actors. I've heard some people say that the plays I write sometimes look slightly odd on the page. They don't necessarily read particularly well but that's because I'm writing knowing what the actors can fill in. I write with an internal rhythm that actors like to find. And they do find it. Just knowing how an actor acts means I can cut the words back. I do that naturally and I do it even more when we get into rehearsal. They'll be playing a scene and I'll think, 'That's just so obvious. He really doesn't need to say it because he's doing it.' I think those things are helpful.

What drew you to work with Shared Experience and how have their working methods influenced the way you prepare an adaptation?

It was accidental. I didn't know anything about Shared Experience. I hadn't seen any of their work. I'd just written my first proper play which was on at the National Theatre Studio. Nancy Meckler was looking for somebody to adapt *Anna Karenina*. I think she felt quite strongly that she wanted a woman to do it. She finds it very hard to find writers who work in the right way for the company and can step beyond naturalism quite confidently. She read my play and took to it because it does go beyond naturalism and it's quite poetic. She asked me to meet her and we got on very well. I hadn't read *Anna Karenina* and she was only halfway through it, but we had a good conversation and I think she felt encouraged. When we'd both finished the book we talked again and we were drawn to similar images, so she asked me to do it. I'd never done an adaptation before so I went to see one of their shows. It was very exciting. I was thrilled by the thought of being able to do anything in a space and that they weren't daunted about creating difficult images on stage, such as Anna's death under the train.

The first thing we did were workshops with a group of actors, which is something Shared Experience always do when they're starting a new project. That essentially consisted of taking bits from the play that Nancy and I felt were really dramatic and jumped out at us, and finding ways of putting them on their feet. Now when I sit down to write, I visualise ten actors in a space. What's good about Shared Experience is that they do get the actors involved right from the start, so it feels organic. And I remember having meetings with the set designer before I'd even started writing. It's a big team, all the different disciplines are rooted very strongly from the beginning, which is rare. It's terrific for me because it's 3D from the start. I really respect Nancy's way of directing and how brave she is; the physicality of everything and the way that quite often a scene can just be an image or a picture. Now that I've worked with her more I can write whole scenes and know exactly what they can do with it. I know how they'll make it work. Shared Experience and my adaptations are inextricable.

Where do you begin with an adaptation? What's your starting point and your basic process?
First of all I make sure I've got the right book to do. I won't just do anything. I suppose what I look for most is a strong inner life in the characters. I like there to be a depth of psychology that I can dig out and turn inside out. With *The Mill on the Floss*, the three Maggies was a way of dramatising that inner struggle. I have to identify with what the writer is saying and feel that what the writer is exploring is important and relevant to an audience. Once I've decided I'm going to do a certain book, I read it several times, research it, read every bit of criticism I can find on it and formulate my own ideas. With *Anna Karenina* and *War and Peace* I went to Russia to talk to Russian experts and visit locations that were relevant. You really have to respect the writer you're dealing with. I don't see the point of doing it otherwise. You have to get behind their philosophy of life. Then I make loads of notes about my thoughts and other people's thoughts. I make notes on every chapter so that I know it inside out, so that I haven't missed a thing.

During all this time, hopefully, some kind of device will have been shaping in my head about how to unlock the book theatrically, for example, in *Anna Karenina*, having Anna and Levin talk to each other was the key to it. Once I'd found that device it meant I could dip into their psychology and move the story on at exactly the pace I wanted it to move. Sometimes that's easier than at other times. *War and Peace* was a bit of a nightmare. *The Mill on the Floss* came quite quickly. Choosing that device usually happens in conjunction with identifying the central theme of the adaptation. I have to know what I'm exploring. I like to see the path quite clearly. I know that if I stick strongly to the central theme, many other ideas will take care of themselves.

Putting it into words, it all sounds a bit clinical, but it's all happening at the same time. It soon becomes apparent what I need and what I don't need from the book and then I start writing. I write the second draft really quickly and there are not usually too many changes. I always try and get it as near as possible first time. Then rehearsals are upon us and it's usually just a question of cutting after that. They're pretty set, the scripts.

How painful is the cutting process to you?
It can be really awful. I always enjoy it at first because we're cutting extraneous stuff and I feel that it's making the script much tighter. I love honing it down, but it always gets to the stage where I feel they're cutting essential things. It's usually two thirds of the way through rehearsals that we have to make some really tough decisions and that can be agonising. But Nancy's particularly good at knowing what can go and when we reach that stage, for the most part, I go with her judgement because I'm too involved to see clearly. Occasionally I will put something back in a published text that was cut from performance. It's my way of getting revenge!

We've touched on this a little bit. In a play you have to show, you can't describe. Do you have to work hard to find dramatic ways to convey complex literary narrative?
I can't be doing with narrators. I think they're so dull and untheatrical, so I always try and find a way of opening it up. The key is finding somebody for the central character to confide in. They need a confidant. Anna's confidant is Levin and vice-versa, so all the things she would have been thinking on her own can be verbalised.

It helps if there's some conflict as well. There has to be some conflict between the confidant and the central character so that the more the confidant pushes, the more the protagonist reveals. With *The Mill on the Floss*, once I'd set up the idea of having the three Maggies, they could really clash and pull everything out of each other. What was lucky was that the first Maggie (the child) was very basic and muscular. For example, she would have huge, dramatic tantrums or imagine she had seen the devil, and I could realise things of that nature without her having to be drawn out by another character. But by the time the story gets more psychologically complicated there are either two or three of them to work off each other.

But you don't lose the sense of Maggie's isolation either, which is remarkable.
Yes. Shared Experience are very good like that. They know that they have to set up a very special atmosphere when those moments take place. When Anna talks to Levin there's a strange sound effect so that you feel as if time has been suspended. Those moments feel very closed and intimate and we know they're not taking place in real time. It's as if we've stepped into the person's head. In *War and Peace* the conversations between Pierre and Napoleon act in a similar way, although because *War and Peace* was so vast and there were so many different characters, it required several different devices. It takes you onto a different plane and allows for a huge emotional pull.

Tolstoy and Eliot are such fantastic psychological writers that it really makes all that possible. It's such a privilege, you know. I end up feeling terribly intimate with Eliot and Tolstoy and they are wonderful people to feel intimate with. It does feel like a privilege when I feel I've understood the layers that were going on in their heads while they were working. With *Anna Karenina* I really felt that Tolstoy had created Anna and Levin as two sides of the same person. It was as if they symbolised the conflict that went on within himself, between following your heart and getting hold of life in all its glory and the desire to live on a higher spiritual plane, denying yourself some of the things you want in order to live a better life and being a good person in the eyes of God. I'm sure he wasn't conscious of all this as he wrote, but I'm sure it was there and to be able to draw those things out in a play is really exciting.

You do create some very powerful, precise and economic stage images to convey essence of meaning. How do you find these and is the biggest part of your work to create these images?
Some things come up in rehearsal, like the use of the cutlery in *War and Peace*. That was something that came out of the actors doing a mime of a social soirée. I think it was Liz Rankin, the choreographer, who spotted the fact that it seemed as if they were using weapons. So that developed from that. Other images are very

much there in the text from the start. That's part of my job as a writer with Shared Experience, to visualise images and write them in, for example the hunched figure in *Anna Karenina* who represents death. I had to visualise how that would work on stage. With something like the battle scenes in *War and Peace* I try my best to visualise how they can work, but I can't always do it completely because those things really have to be physicalised by the actors. We're very reliant on the actors to come up with things, and the choreographer. The flood at the end of *The Mill on the Floss* was so cheeky really because I wrote, 'The flood hits. The actors become the flood. Maggie tries to get to the boat,' and then in rehearsal they had to sort it out.

One of the most difficult things in an adaptation must be to show the passing of time and events have to be much more immediate in a play of three or four hours. Do you feel that you're forced to become more imaginative because you have the practical task of showing an eight-hour story in less than half the time?
Yes, that's really true. It forces you to take more risks. It forces you to become more theatrical. You have to find a device that enables you to move the story along. *War and Peace* was awful in terms of that because it spans such a vast amount of time. You're also trying to fill everybody in on what's happened. When we're in the more domestic scenes and away from the war, you have to keep a sense that the war is still going on and of the big events and battles that have taken place. It's a combination of things. You have to write very deftly. You have to slip references in whenever possible, without it ever being just a simple matter of getting information across. You have to think in the way of, 'Okay, I want there to be an awkwardness between these two characters so perhaps I could use that to get across the fact that one of them supported the French and one of them didn't.' You have to find ways of picking out scenes and situations that can do those things in one swoop. It's very tricky.

What's the difference in your creative approach to an adaptation and to your original writing?
With my original work I'm not constantly thinking about physicality. I allow myself to be slightly more word-bound. I always have a sense of what I think should be going on on stage and there often will be one strong physical idea behind each scene, so they overlap in that respect, but I allow the words to take over a little

more. With the adaptations, the stories that I'm telling are so huge that I cut straight into the nub of what's going on. There isn't much room for building up atmosphere, whereas with my original work there's a little bit more space for that. Although *The Clearing* has a strong narrative and there are similarities, there are also great long scenes where people talk for a long time and that's quite hard to do in an adaptation. I don't have a particular method with my original work. There's no fixed way of doing it.

Do you find it quite liberating to create something entirely fresh?

Yes, I do. It's probably the most satisfying thing you can do. It's more agonising though and I'm not somebody who can write a lot. I'll never write a lot of plays. If I write one original play every five years I'll be lucky because it takes me a long time to brew them up. This is probably too black and white, but writing an adaptation is like scoring a penalty and writing an original play is like scoring a goal. With an adaptation it's all set up for you, there's skill involved and a lot of nerve, but at the end of the day the ball is in front of the net. Although I think of the adaptations as plays in their own right, they are essentially collaborations. I'm collaborating with the person who wrote the novel.

Setting *The Clearing* during Cromwell's barbaric rape of Ireland serves to remind us that we started the problems in Ireland. One critic felt, 'We should be looking forward, not back.' Do you think this comment is symptomatic of our abnegation of responsibility for our part in the troubles?

Well, first of all, yes. It is an abnegation of our responsibility and I think it was a good reminder of the fact that the Irish problem is not the Irish problem but the English and Irish problem. I wrote *The Clearing* at a time when there was a big outcry over the kind of ethnic cleansing that was taking place in the former Yugoslavia. We were all taking this moral high-ground and there was a sense that this is something other countries do. We don't associate it with those tendencies in ourselves. I think any nation is capable of doing that and I wanted to explore those tendencies and where they come from, what they're rooted in. I felt that to do it with a situation where we were the perpetrators would be a good way of bringing people up short. If I'd wanted to write a political play about the situation in Ireland now I would have done it. I'm not running scared of writing a political play.

The Clearing **was praised in reviews, but it was also criticised for being over-lyrical, excessively poetic and emotionally over-wrought. How did you respond to these criticisms?**

I think it's a load of old rubbish. And I was constantly misquoted. They would say something like that and give an example and it would be a complete misquote of the line. It drove me nuts. I think it's something to do with the fact that I'm a woman writer. They thought, 'Oh whimsy, womany play.' *The Clearing*, more than anything else I've written, is often performed in different countries and I think that's because it's lifted out of the everyday. There are no jokes about British telly or *Blind Date* or any of that Englishy, blokesy stuff that we have so much of these days. It has a poetic heart to it and if that's a problem then fine, but it's not a problem for me and it does mean that it becomes more universal. Many more people can identify with it.

The Clearing, **at one level, is a battle between the destructive, non-spiritual, male force and the positive, mystical and older power of the female. Did you see the play like this, perhaps as an analysis of how the new male power attempted to obliterate ancient female power?**

Yes, that's definitely there. It's there in a very practical way in that the Brahon laws that existed in Ireland before we arrived and fucked everything up were much more female-friendly. Females inherited land and there was none of this marginalisation of the woman. It was all much more human. They were for humanity, not for men. So on a very tangible level that's true. Also I feel that a lot of the reason that these sorts of situations occur is through fear. The root of it is fear. Men are more afraid of each other and of life and death than women are. Women are much better at transcending their fear. Men retaliate more strongly and perpetuate fear and it just gets worse and worse. Women have a profound sense of what is really important in life. They have their priorities sorted out better than men do.

In *War and Peace* **and** *Anna Karenina* **you emphasise the unbear-able restrictions that were forced on women. Was it difficult working with Tolstoy's often insensitive treatment of them?**

With *Anna Karenina* it wasn't so difficult, in that I think his portrayal of Anna is really rather wonderful; for a man to have got inside her head in the way that he does. There was much more of a problem with *War and Peace*. I thought the portrayal of Andrei's wife was unfortunate in that he'd chosen to make her a rather shallow, almost stupid person. I know there are shallow and stupid women, just as there are shallow and stupid men but it seemed particularly cruel to pair Andrei who's so arrogant and full of his masculine pride with someone so silly. But I never feel that it's my job to iron out his characters. I don't feel I can do that. Sonya is another he treats badly, somehow implying that it's all her own fault. All I could do really was put in moments that point out their agony. It's so hard because I don't want to change an author's view or perception. It's not my job to do that. If you start unravelling some of those strands it starts off as a little end of wool sticking out and then you end up with nothing. All I can do is play around with the focus and make sure that people's little personal moments are given space.

You have set a new trend in stage adaptations in that your plays remain true to the spirit of the original novel but take liberties to find their essence and as a result achieve much more than a straightforward dramatic retelling would. They stand alone as unique works. Why is it so important for you to adapt in this way and not some sort of purist way?
Because I don't see the point of doing anything in the theatre unless I feel it's got something to say that's useful to us all. I'm not somebody who believes in art for art's sake. I think art has a moral responsibility, so when I adapt something I adapt it not because I want to do homage to the writer or because I think that's a good story, but because I want it to affect people, even if it's only for the time that the audience is in the theatre. I want it to question or alter the way they look at life, to give them a chance to see something from a different perspective and to make us all look at ourselves a bit harder. I think that's really important. The way we all live our everyday lives, and I'm as subject to it as anybody else, is that things are reduced. We live in a shrunken little world of our own, with our own needs and responsibilities. We worry about whether we've got something to wear to that party next week or what we're going to cook for dinner, and what is so fantastic about theatre is that, if it's really good, it can bring us into contact, even if only in a glancing way, with the better part of ourselves as human beings; our bigger selves, our more important selves. That's why I write plays. That's what I'm always striving to do and sometimes it works and sometimes it doesn't. That's the bottom line. I wouldn't bother otherwise.

Winsome Pinnock

Winsome Pinnock is one of Britain's leading contemporary playwrights whose work has been seminally important in giving women and Britain's black population a prominent voice. Her plays explore a host of universal concerns including identity, cross-cultural fusion, integration, poverty and crime, raising complex questions that elude simplistic interpretation. She has won wide acclaim for the humour, honesty and 'simple majesty' of her writing (a fitting accolade given to her by Yvonne Brewster of Talawa Theatre Company.) Born in Islington in 1961 of Jamaican parents, she obtained a joint honours degree in English and Drama from Goldsmiths College and began her playwriting career when she joined the Royal Court's Young Writers Group.

Her work includes: *A Hero's Welcome* (rehearsed reading at the Royal Court Theatre Upstairs, 1986; revised by the Women's Playhouse Trust and runner-up prize in the 1990 Susan Smith Blackburn awards); *The Wind of Change* (the Half Moon and tour, 1987); *Leave Taking* (Liverpool Playhouse Studio, 1988; Lyric Studio 1990; winner of the George Devine Award, 1991; and revived at the Royal National Theatre and on tour in 1996); *Picture Palace* (Women's Theatre Group national tour, 1988); *A Rock in Water* (Royal Court Theatre Upstairs, 1989); *Talking in Tongues* (Royal Court Theatre, 1991, whilst she was Writer-in-Residence under the Thames Television Award scheme); and *Mules* (Clean Break Theatre Company, Royal Court Theatre Upstairs, 1996.)

Winsome's television work includes: *South of the Border* (BBC 1, 1988); *Chalkface* (BBC 2, 1991); and co-writing the Screen Two film *Bitter Harvest* (BBC 2, 1992). *A Rock in Water* is published by Methuen, in BLACK PLAYS 2); *Talking in Tongues* in Methuen's BLACK PLAYS 3); *Leave Taking* by Nick Hern Books, in an anthology entitled FIRST RUN; and *A Hero's Welcome* by Aurora Metro. Winsome is currently working on a screenplay of *Mules*. In October 1997 she was appointed Visiting Judith E. Wilson Fellow at Cambridge University.

* * *

You are one of the very few black women playwrights in this country whose work has been recognised and celebrated by the mainstream. How hard has it been for you to forge a career as a playwright? Have you met with much support along the way?
The Women's Playhouse Trust were really important to my career because although there was good response to my first couple of plays and they were produced as rehearsed readings at the Royal Court Theatre Upstairs, the interest did kind of fade. It was Jules Wright at the Women's Playhouse Trust who really picked up on my work and promoted it in a way that gave it importance. She didn't make apologies and say, 'Well this is just a first play by some new writer,' she said, 'This is a play by a good writer and you really want to see it. It's worth doing.' There was a lot of interest in my work when I first started because it was at a time when the black woman writer was sexy. There were a lot of black, American women novelists and they had become very successful and fashionable. And there was an upsurge in women's writing anyway. There was a big interest in it. So I guess all of that enabled me to do quite a lot of work.

When you first start writing you begin with a passion. You have a lot to say about the world you inhabit, which you feel hasn't been told, especially in the theatre. I had a lot to say about my world, but it becomes more difficult as you mature as a writer and your subject maybe broadens, or changes. Your writing becomes a bit more complicated and the things that you want to look at are not as straightforward. As a writer you're dependent on directors championing your work and if there isn't interest in the sort of work you're doing, you fade out of the picture. Theatre in general is director-led. It's directors who choose what goes on and their response to plays is very personal and dependent to some extent on fashion. And if the trend is for very male plays about masculinity, then you get caught up in that. People go for the safer commercial bet. Women need their work to be looked at and picked up by people who are genuinely interested, organisations like the Women's Playhouse Trust, because to be dependent on men in an organisation is a precarious position to be in. That's the really scary thing, to realise that as a writer, you are dependent on individuals to make the work happen. It doesn't matter how much you write, it has no power if people don't allow it to be heard.

What do you think about the idea that there's an unconscious prejudice against women writers?
It doesn't feel that unconscious if you're a woman. It's so awful because you feel so paranoid and yet you see it happening to other women. They're being faded out of the picture, marginalised. These are complex issues, but there's definitely something happening. In the past people could level accusations of incompetence, but that's not true anymore. It's not to do with the quality of the work. The trend really is for a particular kind of play at the moment and that marginalises every play that doesn't fit the trend.

There must be a great burden of responsibility on you, as one of the only prominent, black women playwrights, to speak for a whole generation, race and sex. Do you ever feel that you have to address certain issues politically even though artistically they might not be a priority on your agenda as a writer?
I want to address certain subjects: the way that cultures collide and the way race and the whole issue of identity presents itself to me in my own life; the different stages I go through in my own life, the different developments I see in various communities that I'm part of. I want to address that, but I do feel that there is a conflict between political intent or a political agenda, if you like, and an artistic one, although often I think that it can be very stimulating. One of the things I've found is that because of the area I'm writing about, I'm sometimes forced to clarify what I'm saying because people don't understand. I find that artistically limiting because writing can't always be clear. You can only express some things in a complex way, or symbolically, and part of it is about not explaining. But on the whole I find the conflict itself interesting. It's an artistic discovery for me. But there's so much to be told that in a way it means that I'm not as free as I could be.

Although all your plays challenge socio-political reality, they are never dogmatic or didactic and the human story is always at the centre as a priority. Is this something you work consciously towards? Why is it important to work this way round?
Because I'm first and foremost a writer and that's what writers do. I think if you weren't a writer you would maybe write the other way round. That was one of the things that was foremost in my mind when I first started writing for the theatre. A lot of the things I saw on stage showed black people representing a kind of anger. I wanted to explore that anger, but the truth of it, so that it wasn't just a cliché or stereotype. I wanted to write about things I'd seen,

observed, witnessed, with some degree of honesty. I wanted to write about the greyer areas of identity. And I wanted to write about women as well because there weren't many black women on stage. You start writing and you do begin with certain ideas; then you just get taken away as the characters become fascinating in their own right.

I think the more I write, the less I want to write about race in the way that I have done and the more I want to write human stories, because I think that our society is becoming so much more hybrid. Cultures are fusing. People are taking on different cultures and there seems to be no reason anymore to consciously state who you are, or shout about who you are. There are other interesting things to write about now. So in the future that's where I'm headed.

In *Leave Taking* the terrible sense of betrayal and disappointment and the pressures of displacement that were felt by the first generation of black people who came to this country is given its rightful stage space, and the tragedy of their experience has a huge emotional impact. Was this something you felt compelled to record in order to promote a wider understanding?
Leave Taking was the first play I wrote. I had started writing about the conflict between generations, between the first-generation immigrants and their offspring and the different ways in which they perceive their identity and how that brings them into collision with each other. At some point during that I was interviewing black soldiers for a documentary about the veterans of the second world war and of the Falklands war. With a lot of the older people I spoke to, their position was so different to the younger generation's. When we looked at their interviews afterwards, we were laughing at some of the things they said which seemed very uncle-Tomist, about treading quietly and behaving themselves and their loyalty to the British Empire, but underneath all that I felt there was a dignity and a real anger as well, that was differently expressed to the younger generation's whose anger was very raw and explicitly stated.

When I started the play, I began with the girls and their confusion, but I became far more interested in their parents' generation and what they'd been through. It was like bearing witness. For me it was quite an extraordinary thing when it had its few performances at the National Theatre last year, to see a woman like Enid centre-stage at the National with the usual National Theatre audience going to watch her. Because when you watch a performance of a play, you are forced to identify with whoever is the heroine at that point. So people were identifying with someone who was seemingly 'other' and yet the feedback I got was brilliant, 'Yes, that's me.' Or, 'that's my mum,' irrespective of their class or race. But that's what theatre does in a way. If you're true to your characters, that's what happens. It does question the idea of universality and what that means because you write specifically about something, but people can identify with it, even if it's alien to their culture. You can enter different worlds. Although I can see there's a fear about doing that sometimes.

Throughout the play you look at the cost that silence from the older generation about their roots, history, traditions and identity has had on a younger, contemporary generation of black people. There's almost a conspiracy from the older generation not to talk about the past, isn't there?
That's based on when I was growing up. If you ask anybody my age they'll say, 'They never told us anything about where they came from, how they lived.' And in *Leave Taking*, in my own life I suppose, the silence was to do with a sense of shame. The sort of poverty they came from was shameful, they thought. And there was a desire for their children to be British, and therefore to forget about the past. I remember being told off if I spoke with a West Indian accent. 'Don't. You're British. Speak English.' I understand that because it's about fitting in, integrating and getting on. If you didn't you'd be an outsider. But the play was about celebrating those things that people were ashamed of. And also for me it was about saying, 'Look, this is who we are. This is what our lives are and were like.'

Viv represents the success story that parents of Enid's generation wanted their children to become, but she sabotages her success by deciding not to take her exams. Why did you want to show her making this decision? Was it a stand against a system and a culture that she had had enough with?
For her there needs to be another journey, which is the journey back, to make her aware, to find herself and then to succeed on her terms. Not to feel that she has lost herself, or denied who she is, in order to fit in, or fit her mother's idea of success. And the whole act of writing the play is about me saying, 'Well, yes. This is the playwright I am. These are the terms on which I write, within a tradition of European playwriting, but about subjects that take in my own heritage, my own past.'

In *A Hero's Welcome* the way in which you structure the two
very different welcomes that Len receives in England and
Jamaica is brilliant. The juxtaposition emphasises the irony that
in England he is treated like dirt, despite his enormous sacrifice,
leaving his homeland to contribute to the war effort, and in
Jamaica he is hero-worshipped for his bravery, despite the fact
that he didn't actually fight. How did the idea for that come to
you?
I was interested in exploring the impact of British culture on these
people at that time. I wrote that play before I did the research on
the soldiers, but again, all these people were saying, 'We really
wanted to take part and then they only used us as ground crew.'
The irony of their desire to serve 'their country' loyally and the
way in which they were denied that is interesting to me. It was
also the first time I'd used patois and I found that so liberating. It
was another voice and it freed me in some way to be myself as a
writer. It was a breakthrough for me personally, because it felt like
I could just do whatever I wanted and say whatever I wanted and
make things up and create these characters and situations. It was
like discovering my voice. I do sometimes feel, though, that it's a
romanticisation of an imagined past and that actually to write about
the contemporary voice is more difficult.

And the structure, did you just hit upon that, or was it organic,
as part of the process of that play?
It was organic. I remember when I was writing that play, waking
up in the middle of the night, thinking, 'Yes. Idea!' It was really
amazing, getting up, writing down the scene and then going back
to bed. There is something about the new, you know, which is
totally liberating. You have a sort of arrogance where you think,
'Yes. This is the most important thing! This is the best thing!' You
don't have any inhibitions.

Do you plan the structure of a play before you sit down to
write?
Not the whole structure. But as I was writing that play I'd sort of
plan ahead of myself. I didn't really know where I was going, but
I'd have an idea for the end, write that, plan scenes as they went
along and then go back and replan the whole thing. I tend to plan
a lot more now than I did then. But there is always that sense of
not knowing where you're going. For me writing is a performance.
You assume all these different identities. It's about trying to hear
the characters, to hear their voices, and capturing that. And there

are specific things, of course, that you want to bring out in each scene.

One of the main themes in *A Hero's Welcome* is betrayal and how people are fooled, tricked, conned and hurt by others, which is most potently shown through Minda's betrayal of Len. Did you want to use these smaller betrayals between lovers and friends, which are big on the human scale, as a metaphor for the even bigger betrayal of Jamaica by Britain?

I was interested in the way a poor girl like Minda will prostitute herself in order to survive. That sort of desperation is often not explored or understood. I remember her being described in reviews as a 'femme fatale'. And I thought, 'What!?' Minda isn't about being a beautiful 'femme fatale'. She's a girl who is surviving, a girl who uses any which way she can. That's why she ends up running away to Britain because that's what she sees will ultimately rescue her from the desperation of her circumstances. So it was more about why some people wanted to come here and the fantasies they had about how they would be treated, than anything else really.

'Anger keeps you alive,' says Red at one point in *A Rock in Water*, and Claudia tells her father and Carole, 'I'll never accept that this is the way things are meant to be, that I have no power.' Was it important for you to dramatise this hope, to show that collective action can produce change, given that we live in an apathetic time?

One of my things in all the plays is examining the idea of the victim. To be black was always to be in the position of victim. I think in all those plays I play with the idea of what a victim is and none of the characters accept that definition of themselves, because they all take action. It's not just about being angry, it's about somehow moving forward. So Minda has her way of doing it, whatever one thinks about it. Enid again, whatever one thinks about her position, is trying to do something for her daughters, trying to save them from the fate of victimhood and the same goes for Claudia. I just hate the idea of being a victim, of being apathetic or just letting things happen to characters or to oneself. It was about exploring that and exploding a stereotype around the issue of black identity.

In *Mules* and *A Rock in Water*, you look at, among other things, the lack of opportunities for West Indian women which forces the characters into denigrating positions. A trained teacher becomes a prison officer, supporting the system that oppresses her, and the 'mules' take on dangerous drug-trafficking work to escape their poverty. Both plays are clearly an angry attack on the system that makes these desperate choices necessary.

It's the victim thing again. I'm interested in the way that people escape that. From the time I spent in Holloway prison, it seemed to me that a lot of the women, so-called criminals, were actually taking action to provide for their families, in the way they knew how. It's very strange, but crime can be a kind of rebellion, a way of empowering oneself, and it's difficult for us to accept that, but it's true. It's also a way of just getting one over on the system. I was interested in what made the women do what they did. It's the same for women higher up in that hierarchy of the drug-smuggling world. They're running away from some kind of limiting way of living or of seeing themselves. They're escaping being victims.

In *Mules* all the women sell their bodies in some way, whether through slave labour or drug-trafficking, and use the money they've earnt to buy clothes and make-up. Success and self-respect, it seems, are defined by how closely they can match that media image of the stereotypical woman and their bodies are the only thing of value.

Yes. It was about how those women didn't question their success and just took on the emptiness of capitalism; on the one hand, sticking two fingers up at the system, in terms of being involved in crime and on the other hand being totally immersed in it; in its values of consumption and exploiting people who are weak. It was simply again what I observed in my research and in the work I did in Holloway. There was a kind of irony in the way that people were rebellious and in another sense conformist and unaware of that conformity.

You didn't see *Mules* specifically as a 'black' play, did you?

No. It's a shame because you know, the play isn't about race and I don't see why reviewers would assume that it was. Even though it was written for a mixed cast and it was played by an all-black cast, I don't see why one can't just see them as characters and that there are other areas being explored apart from race.

All your plays address the disabling problem of an internalised inferiority complex, that black people in the UK are still trying to throw off to some extent. Do you think this problem and the converse superiority complex of many whites are still as

widespread? How can we work towards better transcending these rigid and negative notions?

Yes. All my work when I think about it, has been about that. And it relates to my own position within theatre and the way in which the things I am writing will be valued or not valued, assessed and whatever. There's a long way to go. You see it in a lot of the mainstream theatres, the fact that racial issues aren't really addressed. You know, I go to a theatre and I may see a black woman or man playing a servant and that for me means something. It has repercussions beyond the fictional world of the play because it touches on history and it touches on the fact that we're not addressing history. We have the opportunity to create new ways of being, theatrically. There are so many ways in which a play can be produced. You can cast cross-culturally without even making a statement if you don't want to, by just doing it as a matter of course.

Does it also disturb you that your work is predominantly seen by white audiences and not mixed audiences?

Yes. I want it to be seen by everybody. I want my work to be seen by a mix of people. If you look around at the audience in a theatre like the Royal Court there isn't usually a single black face. It's good when one of my plays goes on because you do get a whole new audience. But they never stay, which is a real shame. They don't come back and watch another play. I don't think they feel they belong there. And in a way they don't because there doesn't seem to be any attempt to welcome different audiences into the theatre, except when a so-called 'black' play is on and then the theatre gets out its 'black' mailing list. It would be nice if they were invited to see everything. The only theatre that's been successful in mixing its audiences is Theatre Royal, Stratford East. And it's such fun to go there. But it would also be quite exciting if we could just see what's happening in society reflected on the stage.

April de Angelis

April de Angelis's highly original plays have explored a range of controversial issues, from pornography and censorship in *The Life and Times of Fanny Hill*, to a woman's tyranny and abuse of power in *Ironmistress*. Ardently socialist and feminist in her early work, her recent plays have moved towards a more complex questioning and re-examination, though her personal politics are still firmly in place. Perhaps her greatest achievement is that her searching explorations always come out of a strong understanding of the theatrical, and wonderful, in-depth characterisation. April obtained a first-class honours degree in English Literature, trained as an actress at East 15 and completed teacher training before dedicating herself to playwriting. In addition to writing for theatre, radio, television and opera, she still regularly teaches playwriting workshops.

Her plays include: *Breathless* (Albany Empire, 1986, winner of the Second Wave Young Writers' Festival, published by Sheffield University Press); *Ironmistress* (Resisters Theatre Company, Young Vic Studio, 1988; published by Methuen in PLAYS BY WOMEN, VOL. 8); *Crux* (Paines Plough Theatre Company, national tour, 1989, whilst Writer in Residence; published by Aurora Metro); *The Life and Times of Fanny Hill* (Red Shift Theatre Company, national tour, 1990; published by Methuen in FRONTLINE INTELLIGENCE, VOL. 4); *Hush* (Royal Court Theatre Downstairs, 1992; published by Methuen in FRONTLINE INTELLIGENCE, VOL. 1); *Playhouse Creatures* (Sphinx, national tour, 1993; published by Samuel French); *Soft Vengeance* (Graeae Theatre Company, national tour, 1993) and *The Positive Hour* (Out of Joint and Hampstead Theatre, 1997).

April's radio plays include: *Visitants* (winner of the Young Writers for Radio competition, BBC, 1989) and *The Outlander* (for BBC Radio 5, 1990, winner of the Writers' Guild Award for Best Children's Radio Programme). She has written three librettos: *Pig* and *Greed* for the English National Opera and *Flight* for Glyndebourne Opera; and a television screenplay, *Aristophanes*, for Bandung and Channel 4, broadcast in 1995.

* * *

The need for constant questioning is a dominant theme in all your work: as Rosa says in *Hush*, 'You have to keep looking, otherwise there's no chance of almost knowing something. The point of the game is not to stop looking.' Was it your interest in the human condition that compelled you to start writing?

You have to keep thinking about things. It's not healthy to get stuck in one fixed way of looking at the world, in fact characters who do that are deathly characters. They're always characters who have to be shaken up or through the play they might have to reappraise their world. If I had to say why I started writing it was just that I really loved it. I'd written one play at university and I can't remember enjoying anything quite as much as doing that. When I left university I wanted to be an actress. I didn't write anything for three years and I really was nagged. Part of me kept saying, 'You must write something.' I didn't consciously think about the human condition then, but you have to develop that side of yourself and think, 'Well, why am I doing this? What am I trying to say?' It's something you have to face in some way as a playwright.

In *Ironmistress* Martha is liberated from financial dependence and caged domesticity when she inherits the ironworks, but her only power model is a male one and she becomes unsympathetic when she in turn exploits Shanny Pinns. Why was it important for you to show this?

All plays come out of a time and a situation. I'd been writing for the women's theatre company Resisters and we were aware that there was a change happening. There had been all these plays about oppression and how women were the victims of a situation, but it was 1988, Margaret Thatcher was in power and you couldn't just write about women as these people who were always blameless. You had to start asking, 'What's a woman really?' I was looking at women and power and that's how Martha, a woman who exploited another woman to get power for herself and who found her freedom through exploiting others, evolved. At the time I would have said she'd absorbed a male role model, a male ideal of power. She was in a situation where the only power available to her was created through patriarchy, but now that just seems naive. There's much more to it. Human beings are very complex and power is desperately hard to handle. Even if you've got the best intentions in the world and you want to implement power benevolently, you

can't. It's hard to ever implement power really well. At a fundamental level, who wants to be told what to do? It's really hard to
take someone else telling you, 'You shouldn't do that. You should
do this.' It's really hard to be Buddhist about it, isn't it? I mean, I
even find feminism telling me what's good for me really hard to
swallow. Now I ask, 'Well what are people like? Does anybody
ever get it right using power?' It's a little bit more pessimistic, but
I don't think it's bad to acknowledge something. It just becomes
more honest and complicated.

**'They're not civilised like us, they don't understand the market,'
says Martha at one point in *Ironmistress* and you show that the
idea of civilisation and market forces can have no real relationship in society. The pursuit of one prevents the other. Can you
tell us more about your thoughts on this?**
That's a classic anti-Thatcher statement and I'd still totally agree
with it. People being allowed to discover who they are, or
expressing themselves, or creating their own ways of being, is
completely at odds with a system that's just about buying and
selling. That's a real socialist statement and I'm still a socialist, but
I don't think it's so simple to dismiss the idea of a market anymore.
People are competitive. It's something you can't just eradicate. My
heart would still be in that statement, but now I'd want to deal
with it in a more complex way. I haven't become a capitalist!

**The church has lost a lot of power and is being exposed more
and more for what it is, with individuals seeking their own
spiritual answers. By focusing on the Doctrine in *Crux*, did you
want to dramatise this shift?**
I remember thinking at the time that if you have a sense of sin then
you can be controlled, because you internalise yourself as worthless.
It's much harder to control people if they feel great about themselves or godlike. The Free Spirits believed that God was
everywhere, so you couldn't have power over them. In the end
ideas can't be controlled and you can't suppress people's instincts.
That's why really oppressive regimes like the one in Beijing have
to be so oppressive if they are going to control people's thoughts.
They have to be rigorous and violent because people don't want to
be controlled in that way. They want to be able to think for
themselves. They have that instinct in them.

What attracted you to adapting *The Life and Times of Fanny*

Hill? **Because you make some very significant additions by introducing the realities of disease and poverty, for example.**

I wanted to choose a novel that was challenging in some way. I'd never heard of *Fanny Hill* but I was looking in my compendium and it said 'Memoirs of a women of pleasure'. I thought, 'That sounds good.' And feminism is traditionally split; some of it's anti-pornography and some is anti-censorship, so pornography is a really big issue.

During the writing of the play I changed my position from being very pro-censorship to thinking, 'Actually what's wrong with erotic material that's meant to excite people?' In fact it's a wonderful thing. Why do people complain that it exploits women? Why don't they attack part-time, low-paid work? Women are exploited in that way so why just attach your anxiety to exploitation around pornography? There is nothing actually wrong with erotic material. It's the way that women are used in the industry that's wrong. That was one side of it and the other thing was that I wanted to show the reality underneath it, so that if you were to allow the people in a pornographic story to be real, what would happen? That's where the other stories came in; so that they weren't just cyphers, one-dimensional figures who had sex. They did have sex, but they also came from somewhere and had a background and a history and you therefore identified with them in some way. I suppose I was trying to do two things: one was to say that erotic material can be life-enhancing and the other, that when you deny the reality of the people working in pornography, then it's exploitative, just like any market forces can be exploitative.

You inverted the usual anti-pornography argument which says that it's men who have the power over these women, by giving women the power.

Yes. They come across as powerful, but in another way they haven't got power; they haven't really got control over what they're doing. They're brought to it by economic necessity, but within that they are not just victims. They've got a business. They help themselves. They know the tricks of the trade. They're very, very accomplished. It's a trade like any other. It's a business. All the world's a market and all the world's a brothel, if you like. Fanny says at the end that everything's for sale, so why just pick on sex? Why just slam sex?

Liberated women are frequently blamed for tearing down the moral fabric of society. You explore this subject directly in the play by highlighting the hypocritical male attitude towards

prostitution and show clearly that the real perpetrators are the clients, who are exempt from responsibility. Was prostitution a metaphor for you to examine the wider question of women and blame?

Yes, but I was making a point about censorship as well and that feminism has often held hands with the idea of censorship, which is even worse. You're holding hands with the people who are repressing women again. The answer isn't to stop grotty material, it's to allow all of us to have a different view of it, so that we're not frightened of it and don't have to repress it or control it. We need a whole different attitude towards sexuality.

Censorship is a big theme in *The Life and Times of Fanny Hill* and, of course, the original novel was banned for many years. Do you think we're currently in a time where censorship of art and the artist is a real threat?

Which ideas are allowed and who's allowed to have them is a big theme for me. I think censorship now comes through lack of funding and things like that. All writers are dependent on the vagaries of whoever runs theatres, except it's often the vagaries of men because men still really do run theatres. In that way the censorship is quite subtle and it still exists for women. But it's not fashionable to ask, 'Why haven't you got any women writers?' You don't want to force quotas because it should be in spirit that they want to give women writers a voice.

You portray the men in *Playhouse Creatures* as cruel tyrants who treat women and animals appallingly and purely as money-making or pleasure-fulfilling commodities.

I was looking at a particular historical period. I wouldn't say that is the state of affairs in theatre at the moment! I was just reflecting the history of the time. The thing that I thought was contemporary and that had relevance was that there are still real limitations put on actresses. Glenda Jackson said there was no *King Lear* for her. You know, you get Ophelia and after that you sort of dwindle into a Gertrude. You don't grow into a Lear. That's what really struck me; the way they were circumscribed in that way and the way that history shrunk the role of those actresses. I didn't know that Nell Gwyn was an incredible comic actress. I just thought she was a mistress who sold oranges. I didn't realise that she had a reciprocal relationship with writers who wrote for her. Why do you only ever hear of her as a mistress? I wasn't trying to make a huge universal statement. I was just looking at those two things really and trying to say that there is a history there that is quite vital and it's a positive thing to know about.

Hush **is quite a departure from your early work and you have said that you wanted 'to ask different questions' and to 'explore my response to Britain today from outside the spectrum of the position of women in society'. Why was this important to you?**
It wasn't that I was rejecting feminism, I just felt that feminism had become very issue-based and I wanted to get away from writing about rape or surrogacy. I think audiences as well were getting tired of seeing things under one umbrella. I wanted to get out of that umbrella and try to address the world without those ideas, whilst somehow taking them with me. It's more freeing as an artist. You don't want to be constrained by any limits. You can't agree to limits and you have to try and be as honest as you can and challenge yourself all the time. You have to write from where you are, don't you? And more and more, now, I think you should respect the characters of the people you are writing, so that you really write about people. Ideas are very important, but at the end of the day you're writing about relationships and people. I think plays are better when they're like that and I wouldn't have thought that that was so significant earlier.

Hush **explored the inadequacy of individual responses and isolated, ideological solutions to the world problems we have today. Clearly individual responses aren't enough and something needs to happen centrally. Do you see a way forward?**
I'm beginning to question those big ideas of capitalism versus socialism. They're a bit simplistic now, aren't they? I believe in humanitarianism, that wonderful, old-fashioned word. It's just more practical and local and respectful of other people.

You have said that you 'write because I want something to be done my way'. Do you still have faith that theatre can inspire people to take action and change?
I do, actually. You go and get moved and you think about something. You watch someone else struggling through something and it makes you more human. I don't think it necessarily means that you'll go out and start a revolution, but it does get you in touch with your feelings as you follow someone else's journey. And it's about people as a group experiencing something and feeling provoked or moved and having those feelings together. It's cathartic

and it grounds you in a funny sort of way. It's also an old and ancient thing, isn't it? It can really inspire you.

Sharman Macdonald

Sharman Macdonald was born in Glasgow in 1951 and graduated from Edinburgh University. She started work as an actress but turned to full-time playwriting after her first play *When I Was A Girl, I Used To Scream And Shout*, which premiered at the Bush Theatre in 1984 (directed by Simon Stokes), brought her overnight success. The play transferred to the West End, was widely acclaimed, won her the *Evening Standard*'s Most Promising Playwright Award and has since been produced all over the world. In 1985 Sharman won a Thames Writer-in-Residence bursary for the Bush Theatre and her second play *The Brave* was produced there in 1988, again directed by Simon Stokes. This was followed in 1989 by *When We Were Women*, which was performed at the Cottesloe Theatre (directed by John Burgess) under the auspices of the National Theatre Studio, and subsequently at the Edinburgh Festival. In 1990 Sharman was commissioned by the English Stage Company to write *All Things Nice* and the play opened the following year at the Royal Court, directed by Max Stafford-Clark. In 1992 *Shades* (directed by Simon Callow), premiered in the West End and was followed in 1995 by *The Winter Guest* (West Yorkshire Playhouse and the Almeida Theatre, directed by Alan Rickman). *The Winter Guest* is currently being made into a feature film, again directed by Alan Rickman, for which Sharman and Alan Rickman wrote the screenplay. Her most recent stage play, *Borders of Paradise* (directed by Lou Stein at the Watford Palace Theatre in 1995) was nominated for the Writers' Guild Best Regional Play award.

Sharman's television work includes: *Mindscape* (BBC Scotland), *The Music Practice* (BBC 2) and *Wild Flowers* (Channel 4). Her radio play *Sea Urchins* (directed by Richard Wilson for BBC Radios 3 and 4), was written for Catherine Bailey Ltd, an independent production company, and has recently been nominated for a Sony award. She has written two novels: *The Beast* and *Night Night*, which are published by Collins. Her first volume of plays: SHARMAN MACDONALD PLAYS ONE (which was shortlisted for the McVities Scottish Writer of the Year prize for 1995), is published by Faber & Faber, who also publish *Shades* and *All Things Nice*. Sharman is currently working on a new play and an opera.

* * *

When you first switched creative direction from actress to writer you wrote only prose, usually in the form of short stories, and turned to playwriting when you discovered that 'dialogue wasn't sacred', after working in television. Was this an important revelation for you? And why were you daunted by the idea of playwriting, especially after having worked as an actress?

I had always written and it had always been prose and it had always been very bad poetry. I worked as an actress, almost exclusively with new plays and new playwrights, and was lost in admiration for the playwrights. Why did I think dialogue was sacred? I suppose at that point I didn't hear voices, so I couldn't write them down. When I write now, I hear what I write. It sounds like a Saint Joan complex, doesn't it? This particular episode of television was quite a long one, and I used to have a lot of time on my own in the rehearsal room, so I would just talk. I'd make up dialogue for everybody who was supposed to be there and just play the whole scene out. I'd write down what I'd said and sometimes other things, story forms with dialogue. That was how it broke through. Obviously I'd improvised before, but not in such a concentrated fashion, and always for somebody else's purpose. It was never just purely on my own and to amuse myself. And there was huge pleasure in it.

Then each time I was on a train, because I was also having to travel to this job, I'd write and it started from there. I decided I didn't want to act anymore, and around the same time my husband made a bet with me that if I sold a script we could have another child. So there was a real push behind it and that was *When I Was A Girl, I Used To Scream And Shout*. I was lucky. I was in touch with what was going on and I think that the play clued into a feeling that there was at the time. I wrote it with purpose, which was that I hated the idea that feminists were putting women up on a platform and that we were 'good' and that men were therefore 'bad'. I wanted to say, 'There are more corners to this than there are straight lines, so let's have a look at the corners.' But with laughter, because it had started from pleasure.

When I Was A Girl explores the sexual repression passed down from mother to daughter and the difficulties of becoming oneself when forced to accept limiting stereotypes from a young age. Do you think this pressure is still as strong?

Well, oddly enough the initial impetus for those scenes came from a boy, my son. I was sitting at the table writing the scene on the beach and he and his friend went upstairs behind me, and what I heard was him talking to his friend about willy games, and I actually wrote down what they said as they passed. There is a tremendous accidental quality to everything because it's a mixture of memory, experience and the immediate. They all feed into it. And is it repression? If they were all playing those games, then what was so repressed? I also felt hugely for the mother because what Fiona did to her, I thought, was absolutely appalling. But what the mother, in turn, was doing and had done was equally appalling. They were repressing each other. Kids aren't born blank. I think they're more often than not born wicked and they express it beautifully and it's wonderful and let's not squash all that. And the games are played anyway. The mother doesn't stop them because they're always played in secret, which makes them sacred, magic and much more fun.

I've always found that there's a huge masculinity in the creatures I write, the more vibrant women: like Pearl in *Shades*, like Morag [in *When I Was A Girl, I Used To Scream and Shout*] to an extent, like Elspeth in *The Winter Guest*, like Rose in *All Things Nice*. There's a kind of drag queen quality to them which is taken from the women I knew when I was young. I've often thought that my feminism actually came from a fear that I would never be as good as they were. You know, they went out to work; their lips were bright red; their nails were painted; their hair was usually dyed; they wore high heels, straight skirts, clip-clopped down the road, baked apple tarts, gypsy creams and victoria sponge cakes – every single week. Their windows were shined with newspaper and, in my case, she sent me to a fee-paying school. *She* paid for that. So their input to the house was huge. And they were women who never, ever thought that there was any need for a feminist movement at all. My mother scorned it because she was the power, as my grandmother had been before her.

So, sometimes I think that my feminism is there because I can't do all that. I can't do what they did. Their vitality and vibrancy was formidable. That's why I ran away from it. My house is covered in dust, I never clean the windows and the Indian take-away sees me far more often than the baking trays do!

In all your plays you explore the hate as well as the great love between mothers and daughters, which makes your women

much more human in that they are clearly flawed. Why is this
so important to you?

Just because we are flawed and we have to forgive ourselves and
other people for the flaws that are there. And if we think that we're
right, then we don't forgive and we don't appreciate and we take
stances and it's all much more complicated than that. You can't
divide into good and bad. You can't do that. It's much more complicated and I like the complication.

You have said that you are 'fascinated by failure and the desire
for it'. Can you tell us more about this?

Yes. I'm also fascinated by success, but I don't know how you
define it. I also don't know how you define failure. I've come up
with 'negative achievement' recently and I could spend my whole
life doing it too. The negative achievements are just as valuable as
the positive ones, so actually it's a method of always succeeding. I
am fascinated by it. There's part of the Scottish nature that desires
failure. Like the Scottish football team who just when they were
lauded to the skies would lose. And you knew they weren't going
to win because the whole of Scotland was sitting on their shoulders.
The honour was too great to bear. But there was a huge heroism
and sentimentality in the failure because you could talk about
it far more than celebrating their success. There was something
embarrassing about the success, but the failure, goodness, you could
glory in it for the rest of your life. I'm sure it's part of the heritage,
part of the land itself. I can't escape it, although I have now lived
more of my life in England than I have in Scotland, but it's still
there, hugely.

In *When We Were Women* you explore human fallibility against
a backdrop of war, and paint, with great compassion, a world in
which we cannot help but fail to meet ideals. You also show the
pain which Maggie and Mackenzie suffer in trying to come to
terms with their imperfections. Do you feel that as a society we
need to become more accepting and less rigid in our expectations
of people? Was that partly why you wrote the play?

Yes it was. It was also to do with the reaction to *When I Was A
Girl*. Some people felt that I hadn't been wholly fair to the mother.
I was appalled by that and so essentially what I wrote in *When We
Were Women* was Morag's background. The story is actually true,
so it was also something that was very close to me, which I felt
had to be explored. Again it was the 'nobody is bad' thing. One
of the speeches that lives in my memory is Maggie's, 'What about

what I want?' On the face of it, what she does is appalling, rejecting her daughter's child and forcing the daughter to have the child adopted, when actually she was at home and why couldn't she have taken it and let the girl go out to work? But she'd had five kids. So you're balancing everything up and saying, 'Let's admit human frailty.' I just wanted to examine that background; Isla was called Isla and not Morag, but I wanted to look at the baggage which Morag had on her shoulders, which none of us can shed, and which made her react to her own child the way she did. I'm very caught by a causal chain and sometimes I think I'm over-faithful to that, but it's there and you can't look at a person separate from their past. Would that we could sometimes. But it was a dangerous thing for me because I really got sucked into it. I couldn't keep away from the production and in order to move on to the next thing, in order to retain balance as a person, I have to sit down and write. If I get sucked into past work there's no balance. I wanted to be near it all the time, but I also had to write. If you get involved in your past work you can't create anything new because the rhythms stay in your head. There's no possibility of the vital coming through again.

Is it your favourite play?
No, it isn't. The favourite is usually the one I'm writing at the moment. They become indistinguishable from the experiences you had while they were going on. But you know that big buzz, that trembling joy you get when you're actually writing something? That's what you do it for, I think, and that buzz is usually attached to the thing that is being created. The joy of the past is a reflective one. The present is charged. And the dreadful depression when you finish something. It doesn't matter if it's going on or not. You think the one thing you want to do is get to the end of it because you've got a deadline or whatever, but the most dreadful thing happens when you do. You expect it to be a lift and it isn't. There's nothing pulling you anymore. The only way to get back to that place, where that excitement is possible, is to create something new. But the doubt and the terror that nothing new will ever occur again, that my creativity would fail me ... I don't know what I'd do. It's a terrifying feeling and it makes for humility.

In many ways _When We Were Women_ is your bleakest play spiritually, suggesting a harsh universe in which God/fate plays tricks with the lives of humans and shows little or no concern for their plight. What inspired this?

I feel like I've been waging war against whatever that word represents. I'm quite militant with my children about belief in a superior being and I knock it all the time. I wonder sometimes why I'm so angry about it. It might simply be that the image of God that I have is confined to a purple-faced man with red hair, leaning over a pulpit and shouting at us every Sunday. It sort of seeps in there somewhere. I don't think I do it as much now, but still the language that the plays are expressed in refers to 'Oh my God', or whatever. It's always part of the structure of the play.

And the notion of prayer: fear produces such sideways movements. I remember a story an English teacher told us of a man on a raft at sea, who'd been dropped out of a plane and who was an atheist, praying to God. And when Mackenzie's talking to God, he is running away from the bombs, and then his brother. He's always *in extremis* when he's doing it. The desire for that supreme being, the desire for comfort, is still in a lot of us, no matter how rationally we reject the notion of it.

In *All Things Nice* you extend your usual exploration to three generations of women and to the grandmother–granddaughter relationship. What interested you about this? You break a big taboo with the idea of a grandmother almost prostituting her granddaughter.
But the grandmother has no knowledge of any taboo. She's not doing anything wrong in her eyes. It's only we who say, 'You were wrong there.' The captain was in her house. He had money. The granddaughter needed money. So what was the sensible thing to do? He was drunk. He wasn't going to be able to harm her. Do people do what they think is wrong? More often than not they do what they think is right. The thing of baggage was still there because I wanted to look at the relationship between the mother and the daughter with the grandmother there. It was a 'What if?' It feeds back to *When I Was A Girl*. If Morag had gone abroad what would have happened? It's odd because I felt there were things that still needed exploring. I couldn't move on. I've always felt that if I could get beyond that barrier what I'd write would be glorious, but I've never got totally beyond it. And with *All Things Nice*, I thought, 'Well if I just write this, then maybe the barrier will come down.' I'm just writing the same play over and over again!

In most of your work, the husbands and fathers have either died or left. Does their lack of presence explain the hunger for male approval that is felt by so many of your female characters?

Yes. I would think it does. I experienced male absence. My father was an engineer and he went to all the various power stations and was away a lot. Latterly we moved around the power stations when he was there, but my mother was a vibrant personality, so my father learnt to be silent. I don't think he started out that way. So the voices that I hear are for the most part female ones, simply because my father was so silent. And because my husband was away a lot on tour and I was at home with the kids, the companionship that I had was again essentially female. The new voices that were coming in were female as well.

And then watching . . . I don't think I've ever flirted in my life. I really regret that. I have watched other people flirt and the glorious way in which they do it, I just envy it so much. I suppose part of my hunger for male approval gets expressed through my writing. I love watching people flirt. I love the colour that's in it, and my plays are written from what I see and hear. I'm an observer, I suppose. There's a distance to it. It's funny because I do sometimes think it's very dangerous, you know, to sit in a room and write, that it's a protection, a way of not taking part in life and getting your hands dirty and that the healthiest thing to do would be to stop, to go out there and wrestle with it, rather than being the observer. A lot of the time I'm being that bloodsucker that I write about, because I'm sucking on other people's lives. I was up in Scotland and one of the guys I was with said to me, 'You're a great listener, you know,' and I had to say, 'Look, this is business.' That's what I feed off. If I don't listen, I can't write. It's all feeding, sucking. Okay, you're doing it in order to explore something, in order to open something up, but actually, the pleasure you get from it makes it slightly questionable.

But as a society we do need mirrors.
Oh yes, that's true. There's a hunger; I don't know if it's a hunger for a mirror, I think it's a hunger for make-believe and we just categorise our make-believe. Some has more class or status than others, but it's all make-believe. It's all the fireside tale and the voices telling the fireside tale, whatever medium it's in. People like me exist because that hunger exists.

You usually use a mother–daughter relationship as the central exploration of your plays, but in _The Winter Guest_ you also focus on a group of young people who are facing their future and two old women who are confronted with the end of their

lives. This makes for an encompassing play in which death is also present as a reality for all. Why did you decide to do this?

Because I was living amongst it. It sounds as if everything I write is autobiographical and indeed it is, but it also leaps with the imagination. I've never met those two old women. I've never known them in my life and they were such a gift. They were in my screenplay *Wild Flowers* too and I couldn't let them go. I had to hear more of what they wanted to say. They were such a joy to write. We'd been living with old people very present and obviously with my children, so the generations had been dancing around me and that was necessarily reflected in *The Winter Guest*. I just wanted to juxtapose. I wanted them all there, because that's what it is, that's life.

You broke a lot of new ground with structure in *The Winter Guest* by creating a piece that was perhaps closer to a dance or a four-part symphony than a 'traditional' play. What inspired you to do this? And did you meet with any resistance in the rehearsal room?

None, because the project started with Alan Rickman, it's still with Alan Rickman and he is one of the best people to work with on a script because what he asks you to do is explore. He accepted the dance. Dialogue is music. I love music and that's why *The Winter Guest* went as far into that, the musical expression of it, as it possibly could. I'd written my film *Wild Flowers* and it was made, but I began to suspect that nobody would ask me to write a film again, so half of me thought, 'Well, okay, I'll experiment with a filmic structure on the stage.' The extraordinary thing is that the stage has so much more freedom than film ever has. It's obvious, really, because film is literal and the stage can be anything. When I came to adapt the stage play into the screenplay I felt I'd gone into a prison because what you couldn't have, not in wintertime, was the action inside the house and the action on the beach at the same time. I was in despair because when I accepted the commission that didn't occur to me. A way round it had to be found and it sent me right back to the stage.

You are very successful as a woman playwright, one of the few who has met with West End success, and now *The Winter Guest* is being made into a major feature film.

Yes, it's wonderful. The West End was wonderful, but that was then and this is now and who knows what will happen in the future. There is a whole new world of film opening up which I do love, despite the fact that I find it constricting. To actually be there with all those people on a set and the focus, the ability . . . oh, I don't know if I do like that – that the camera directs the focus of the audience. Actually I'm not sure I don't prefer it when the actor directs the focus of the audience.

But it's interesting and I like the challenge of it. I've been very fortunate. I don't think there are any rules. I think, generally, audiences still accept the male structure of a piece more readily than they do the female structure. And if you say, 'Okay, the male structure is more orgasmic and the female structure of a piece of drama is more cyclical and the lines go through the female structure like that' (*she makes an interwoven gesture*), audiences don't accept that as readily. There are female playwrights who write to the male structure and audiences accept them more easily. Now, I don't think I do, therefore I am lucky. They accepted *The Winter Guest*, but there have been troughs where they haven't understood. There will be a woman who breaks through it all and will be accepted for the plays that she writes, which is what's important.

There are astonishing women coming through now and it's wonderful. Perhaps it's because we, as a generation, have ceased to blame them for being angry. To an extent I wasn't allowed to be angry when I was growing up because anger was bad. And I'm sure I'm not alone in that. I encourage my daughter's anger and her spirit and I assume that other people are doing the same thing to their daughters and that the generation coming up will be astonishing. Maybe one to shelter from, but astonishing. But not fighting for feminism, that won't be it; they'll simply do and they'll simply be, which is fantastic.

The Scotland you present in your plays is a world of stark, natural beauty, but also one of repression, frustration and small-mindedness; yet invariably you always come back to this world and its people. Is your love–hate relationship with Scotland still as intense? And are you now keen to explore more of other worlds, as you did in *Borders of Paradise* and *The Brave*?
Well I thought that *Borders of Paradise* would lead me into exploring other worlds, but I've gone back to Scotland. God help me! I think I live in little Scotland. Even Mrs James who lives across the road and has stolen my cat is Scottish. My best friend who lives round the corner is Scottish. I'm never going to get away from it. I love it but I think, 'Jesus Christ!' at the same time. Is it just this part of Teddington? Do I attract it? Is it me? I think I'll always return because it's ever-present and because the Scottish

voice entrances me. There's a rawness there, a texture. There's an emotional availability within it that I can't let go of. I think it's the way I'll always express myself.

And there's a lepidopterist in me that wants to pin the moments and pin the language, pin this, that and the other, partly so that I never have to do it again and partly so that it's there. Because there's such richness around us that just flips by, just goes, and you want to have those moments preserved. Like my mother (and she used to get very cross with me for doing it), but I'm so glad that some of her is there, for other folks to laugh at and enjoy and curse, because although every single character is not her, it's to her that I owe a lot of what I've done. It hasn't just passed by and not been noticed.

Charlotte Keatley

Charlotte Keatley's career as a theatre practitioner has been extraordinarily wide-ranging, taking in nearly all the disciplines and providing a rich base for her work as a playwright. After obtaining a Masters Degree in Theatre Arts from Leeds University, she worked variously as a performer, director, co-deviser (with Impact Theatre and Royale Ballé, a three-woman performance art company which she set up in 1984), in community theatre (where her work included writing a community play for Warrington in 1985), as a lecturer (she was Junior Judith E. Wilson Fellow at Cambridge University in 1989), arts editor and theatre critic (for the *Yorkshire Post*, the *Financial Times* and BBC Radio 4's *Kaleidoscope*), before turning her full attention to playwriting. Her ground-breaking first play *My Mother Said I Never Should*, which charted the lives and explored the relationships between four generations of women, premiered at the Contact Theatre, Manchester, in 1987 and went on to jointly win the George Devine Award in the same year, before transferring to the Royal Court's main stage in 1989. It has since been translated into seventeen languages, performed internationally, is an A-level set text and is widely celebrated as a landmark play, not only because of its content, but because it uses an unusual, highly effective, non-linear structure. The play was most recently revived by the Oxford Stage Company and opened at the Young Vic in May 1997 as part of a national tour.

Charlotte has also written musical plays (including *The Iron Serpent*, Theatre Workshop, Leeds, 1983) and plays for children (including *The Singing Ringing Tree*, Contact Theatre, Manchester, 1991). Her television work includes: the children's play *Badger* (Granada Television) and *Falling Slowly* (for Channel 4). Her radio work includes: *Citizens, Is Green The Same For You?* and an adaptation of Mrs Gaskell's novel *North and South*, all for BBC Radio 4. In addition, Charlotte regularly runs creative writing projects, which have taken her from primary schools to universities and from Moss Side (Manchester) to New York and Rajasthan. *My Mother Said I Never Should* is published by Methuen, who also publish a student edition

with commentary and exercises by her. She is currently working on two
new stage plays and lives in Manchester.

*   *   *

**You've worked variously as a performer, director, teacher and
theatre critic, as well as a dramatist. How much have these
experiences informed your playwriting, and does this make you
a different sort of writer?**
I can't imagine writing plays for the theatre without having tried
all the different components; I mean, not just acting, directing or
design, but trying to sell the tickets or make the poster – because
it's such a collaborative art form. I know and understand, or respect,
the vocabulary of the other people coming in and making the
play and I'm not intimidated. It's given me confidence. And that's
particularly important with a new play. I really think a new play
should have a new structure or something about the way that it's
written that's new, but the problem is that often directors who have
got an enormous amount of experience don't believe what you're
doing could work, not necessarily out of a prejudice or an anta-
gonism, but because they haven't seen it before. So I was able to
look after myself a lot better when I started to be a playwright.

My Mother Said I Never Should **has been hugely successful, both
artistically and commercially. In fact, in many ways, your whole
career has been solidly made by that play. Why do you think
this is? Because that's quite an extraordinary thing to have
happened, isn't it?**
Yes it is. I was so happy when I was writing the play. I thought,
'So this is why I've been trying to make theatre.' The territory of
this play matters and it matters to a hell of a lot of people. Not
just women, but men as well. I believed this when I was writing
the first draft. I've worked on it over subsequent years so some
things have changed, but the time-structure and the child scenes
were there and some of the scenes are completely unchanged since
that first period of writing, which was an intensive ten days to
three weeks. The feeling wasn't one of 'Oh I am writing something
that is going to launch me', just that I'd somehow managed to
frame areas of life that I thought were important, that we wanted
to see on stage and explore in the theatre. When it was on at the
Royal Court, no one had heard of me or this play, but it got
the most phenomenal advanced bookings. I can't work out logically
why, but I think people sniff something in advance of seeing it,
something about the substance, a sort of need. I won't write a play

unless I believe that there's a need for it, so I'm a very slow writer and I don't produce much.

Do you consider *My Mother Said* to be a political play?
Yes. Because it's about how people live and what choices they make and what possibilities there are. But then I do think theatre is a political arena, so people who say their plays aren't political are fudging it or missing the point. Max Stafford-Clark, I must say, was great like that. He was, of course, a key decision-maker in putting this play on at the Royal Court and he would say, in committees and discussions, 'Look, this is a play about society.' He was great in seeing that about my work and that of a lot of other women; that they were big plays about society and they needed a main stage. I don't know what's happening at the Royal Court at the moment. The current vogue for American film criteria quite alarms me. All the plays seem to be called 'Sex and Violence' or something close to that. Plays like *Mojo*. Yes, so Jez Butterworth can write great, wacky dialogue, but it's yet again another play about a bunch of men doing nothing much. I'm glad he's found success, but it does piss you off that there's this endless lineage, going back through the centuries, of men writing plays about men doing nothing much. And they are always perceived as being plays about life. Nobody ever reviews them as just being plays about some men in a room. But I've had the comment over the years and even recently about *My Mother Said* that, 'It's about nothing. It's only about four women.' So what is *Waiting for Godot*?!

To me, a new play is always about changing the metaphor. The problem is, women's work is not yet seen as a metaphor in the sense that if we go and see *Hamlet* we don't think, 'This is just an adolescent play for men who feel a bit lost.' We think, 'This play is a metaphor for all of us.' That will partly change just by having more and more plays by women. We've got to flood the market.

You were criticised at the time *My Mother Said* was first produced for presenting a 'lopsided view of the world' because you used an all-female cast. What were your feelings about this?
There's a sort of hysteria among the critics that is so blatantly about their unease that you can't really take it seriously. Seeing the stage swamped with the culture of women, which is unfamiliar to these men, is just too frightening. They don't know how to articulate what they're seeing, how to wrap it up in their understanding of the world, how to use their kind of English on it. Having been a theatre critic myself, I think sometimes you go and see a play that

is beyond the boundaries of what you can respond to in the usual form of criticism, and what you should do, if you're honest, is say, 'I don't know how to describe this play, how to say to you what it's about, but it disturbed me. Why don't you go and see it?' You don't as a critic have to like it in order for it to be good, but that's a kind of honesty and humility that doesn't go with the convention of being a critic, on the whole. I think Sarah Daniels, of all of us, has suffered the most in that respect, because what comes out of her plays is so powerful and uncompromising that there are some male critics who are just scared. They want it to go away. The unconscious part of theatre is at work here as well, something is coming up from a female unconscious, if you like, that is too threatening and too daunting. I also think it's still true that men in this country are brought up not to express emotions or regard it as important as expressing thoughts. The extraordinary emotional content, emotional power of these plays by women is still seen as, 'Please, don't make such an emotional mess all over the stage.'

The interesting thing is that I don't think reviews have any effect on the long-term future of a play. Having said that, I suppose reviews have more of an influence on the commercial lives of plays than they used to in this country and they can stop a play getting a bigger stage. But what I think is so exciting about the response to a number of the plays written by women in the last ten or twenty years is that they are popular with audiences and they keep getting put on in other places because they've got this quality, because they've got this energy and this culture that hasn't been seen much on stage before: a humour, sexiness and wit that's been missing.

Do you think things have improved at all?
Well I do, but it's not very visible, because in this country the media is mostly based in London and it's still very male-led in its language, in what's regarded as good or fashionable. Here's a good example: Michael Billington, who I think is a great ally to new playwrights in a lot of ways and it doesn't matter if it's work by a woman or a man, recently published a book of collected reviews from his last ten or twenty years. I think *Serious Money* and *Light Shining in Buckinghamshire* are the only plays by a living woman in the whole collection. It's almost perverse. I was discussing this with him at a conference and what had essentially happened was that he, or somebody else, had weeded out everything that didn't seem to be the next real step in culture. There are important, key plays from the last two decades written by women, but when it

comes to the crunch those are left out of the line-up. A book like
that, to other people around the world at this moment and to
people in thirty years' time, says, 'The theatre has been constructed
by men, directed by men, in this particular kind of language,
covering these parts of society. These are the milestones. These are
the representatives of our society.' And that's not actually what's
happening in the theatre and it's not what's happening outside
London either, but that's what's written in stone. The problem is
that most people will believe that and it happens so easily because
all institutions and all our constructs in education, medicine and
everywhere else are still so much tipped towards men rising up
and getting a voice and women not.

**You have said that My Mother Said is not a feminist play and
yet the messages in it are very clearly against self-sacrifice,
repression and oppression. What did you mean by this?**
Well, I think it is a feminist play. The problem with the word
feminism is it's very rarely defined by the people who want to call
themselves feminists. It's defined by everybody else as meaning,
'She doesn't shave her legs. She doesn't like men,' or 'She writes
things that haven't got any good parts for me.' When I said that
the play wasn't feminist what I meant was that I didn't want it to
be limited to the idea that it's politically, socially angry in the way
that 'feminist' has come to mean. I like the word 'female'. It feels
like something far older than feminism. I mean, people have been
making theatre for thousands and thousands of years and if you
can start to make theatre in which not just the verbal language, but
the physical language, the imagery, the pace, the subtext, are true
to ourselves, then that's 'female' if you like, rather than 'feminist'.
And with the first production, where by chance all the stage crew
seemed to be women as well, the sense of female magic was extraordinary. We were making this play that was covering things that
we hadn't been able to say in theatre before – and the energy!
When a good piece of theatre really works, it's greater than the
sum of its parts, it's greater than the energy of all the people. You
get slightly exhilarated by that because you can feel it happening
and so can the audience, of course. But in terms of how this play
connects to the age we live in, its political nature, I would say, 'Yes.
It's feminist,' because I think feminism is about the possibility for
all of us to change the roles we've been ascribed. Men as well as
women.

You have said that you began writing My Mother Said by

building the structure in your head and writing in the languages of light, colour, environment and sound, before applying words. Is that how you always work? And why do you use this method?
If you think of the first piece of theatre you ever saw, the first piece of theatre that stays in your head, your memory is always of an image, or an action, or gesture, and you remember that long, long after the words. It enters you like a dream and stays in your consciousness somehow all your life, because it's a metaphor that carries many meanings at once. No line of dialogue can carry as many multiple meanings as that moment in the theatre when suddenly you see a face, a light, a gesture, a colour, an image, all combined. So, it seems to me, you have to devise those for your play. Those are where the meaning, the storytelling and the impact lie. And you may not even be able to explain or analyse them in words and that's fine. You have to get those right and construct dialogue to enable the actors and the audience to get to those images, to recreate them. What I find astonishing is that if you get the dialogue right, without any stage directions or anything, people will produce exactly those images. It makes the hairs go up on your head, but it happens I think, if you are completely immersed as the writer, in the sensory, three-dimensional experience of making a play.

Personally, I can't write anything unless I get physically inside the age or type of that person, that moment. If I write from that point of being, the total experience will somehow be embedded in the spaces between the words. So from the very beginning you try to let your subconscious come up with images, images that you don't really understand, which are frightening, but they are the hunches I go on and those are the images that, when everything else has faded, people will remember.

Is that what you meant when you said that 'theatre is capable of speaking directly in the language of the unconscious'?
Yes. Theatre isn't intellectual. You don't need intellectually to understand, analyse or talk about what's happening, and I think between the writer, actor and audience, that's quite well understood. Our tradition of directors, such as it has developed through this century, muddles that up, because a director these days feels required to have an intellectual, theoretical, analytical, psychoanalytical, politically informed interpretation of a play and announce that to the rehearsal room and to the journalists in interviews, and sometimes the actors frankly just get on with it, you know.

And we're also losing directors who are very good at new plays because of the situation that a director can make their name on a wild interpretation of Marlowe and go up the Snakes and Ladders to the next square at the RSC, but the director of a new play isn't going to get quite the same attention or be given that *auteur* status. You can spend years trying to find a director who relates intuitively to the play, a director who has a sense of the play and an attachment to it which isn't intellectual. I think the journey for a new play, coming in one door of the theatre and having to get through literary managers, directors and committees to someone who will really enable it to come off on stage at the other end, is quite dangerous at the moment. We're possibly losing the most innovative new plays because of this current process, particularly plays by women which don't fit with male-established conventions of theatre. *My Mother Said* was rejected initially by several experienced directors who told me it didn't have a structure, and wasn't about anything. Fortunately I didn't give up, and Brigid Larmour understood the play as soon as she read it. (She directed the first production.)

Do you think most plays fail to tap into the power of the unconscious?
I think playwrights aren't encouraged enough at the moment to go for that. We live in such a media age, don't we? It's very fast-moving, so every week a whole bunch of films, plays, books and albums get reviewed then hurled aside for the next wave to come in. I don't think theatre works successfully at this pace at all, as an art form; this pace is not about acknowledging the unconscious or the things we can't immediately analyse.

You've talked about women having evolved a 'female aesthetic' in theatre writing, one that's not linear.
Yes. I'm just trying to think why it happens that quite often, in contemporary plays by women, time doesn't go chronologically. It doesn't just go forward. We seem to be able to refer sideways and backwards at the same time and understand that that's not confusing, but very useful. I mean, if you were to write down now, on the spot, the most important event in your life so far, just whatever comes into your head, and then the next most important event and then the next, chances are that the list wouldn't be chronological at all. Most of us instinctively, when we're writing our personal histories, don't use the chronological, linear time that history books and the news would have us believe is the correct and true way of doing it. The order is dictated by what you need

to tell. And this is a pattern that various plays by women seem to follow and it's completely recognisable to all people of both genders actually, it's just that it hasn't been backed up, so far, in our art forms or on our bookshelves. It's not one that's generally used, so the people who are using it at the moment, who happen to be women, have a problem getting that recognised as a valid means of constructing a play. You literally get told, 'This is not a play. This is not how you make a play.' There are male writers, like Anthony Minghella, who use that, it's not just exclusive to women. Throughout the eighties plays by women did this, particularly those that were staged at the Royal Court, and they have now influenced the ways in which men, as well as women, are writing. The younger generation have consciously or unconsciously absorbed that. But it's not something that's recognised.

You were very clear that you didn't want the set for *My Mother Said* to be naturalistic, but rather 'a magic place where things can happen'. What freedoms did this allow for?
I don't go to plays to see furniture, that's why I said, 'No sofas in this play.' I've been an actor and what you want to do is use your whole body to communicate with an audience and if somebody has you sitting down through most of Act One, well then you've lost half your capacity to express things. I like the idea that there's space. And part of that comment is also about 'Let's prioritise that theatre is about human beings going through transformations'. I think that is what is at the heart of what plays can do, re-enact transformation. I think playwrights are shamans and you've got to hold on to that.

What I do when I write a play is set up an experiment, you know: 'Let's look at these people and now watch, they're going to change in front of your eyes into something else.' And we experience alongside all the most wild, fascinating, frightening and exciting ideas of how we might change our lives in an instant – and how we can, and how easy it is to do. So if your theatrical conventions don't rely on lots of scenery, props, wigs, make-up and everything else, but in the simplest, quickest form show how you can change yourself in time and age and physicality, then I think it feeds back to the audience; that notion that at any moment, during any day, you could actually change completely. And that it's the people around you, the society you're in, that is probably inhibiting you from realising that potential. So my comment is a desire to clear the decks and make theatre about what I think it's really for.

The play explores the lives of four generations of women and allows us to see how traditions and limitations are passed down. What was your reason for choosing such a time span?

Because these are four generations in which women's lives have changed more radically than ever before. It's as far back as you can see, to our grandmothers' childhoods, if you like. Women's lives had changed so little until the beginning of the twentieth century; then there was the effect of two world wars, contraception and everything else. So suddenly there was this radical change in each generation and that's clearly very dramatic if you're a playwright. And four is a good dynamic on stage, I think. Two is very limiting because you can only talk to each other or turn your back and three is very, very powerful and I use that in lots of scenes. Like a dance they move around. But four means that you can have two counts of two, compatibilities between two generations that are not understood by the others. And then you can have three people, apparently ganging up on one, for example, when Jackie gets it in the neck from the three others at certain moments. They all put pressure on her and that's much more powerful than if you just had two generations attacking Jackie. It's the very basic end of theatre: 'What are we going to build this story with?' Numbers, spells, rituals.

The play's web of guilt, frustration and secrecy is finally broken by Rosie when she manages to complete her game of solitaire. Solitaire is a wonderful symbol for independence. Where did the idea come from?

I never put something into a play to be symbolic and I almost feel that if I'd recognised how incredibly symbolic the solitaire game is, I wouldn't have dared use it. In a purely practical way, it's a game which is very much from Doris's period, the sort of old game that Rosie would find and dig out in her great-grandmother's house and wonder what it was. It's a simple object to have in a play where the object language is very ordinary but important. It fits into the vocabulary. And it works as a piece of action. You can analyse its symbolism in endless ways and all of them are right. People always say to me, 'Does the solitaire board mean this?' And I say, 'Yes.' If you get something in a play, which as well as its practical application and usage in that scene also has a symbolic resonance, then whatever symbolic meaning it has is right. An element of a play, once it's enacted on stage, somehow has an energy that's far greater than its apparent, tangible meaning or existence.

The solitaire board works like that. It suddenly spins off and connects with all sorts of other things. When it's a final image on stage, I did put in a stage direction that the other three women appear, because I didn't want it to be an image of isolation. The moment Rosie solves it, Margaret and Jackie and Doris appear on stage, in other times and places, from different moments in their lives. The whole image is not just Rosie solving the solitaire, which would be, 'When I leave the others and am on my own I can do it,' it's the image of this woman, at this moment, in this century now, finding her culture: her female inheritance, and strength. And those other people are as much a part of why she, in this present moment, is able to do this. That one image actually draws together most of what the play is about, which is that we, in this very moment, in this room, are being influenced healthily and unhealthily by all sorts of other things, and particularly for us as women, by women who have gone before.

Clare McIntyre

Clare McIntyre grew up in Woldingham, Surrey, and worked extensively as an actress in repertory theatre (where her roles included playing Dawn in Nell Dunn's *Steaming*) and film (including *The Pirates of Penzance* and *Krull*) before focusing on full-time playwriting. Shrewd, humorous, imaginative and popular, her work successfully captures the preoccupations and anxieties of contemporary women and the complications of human relationships today, exploring, among other things, the heartache and confusion of trying to match up to the physically perfect, the destructive effects of pornography, middle-class discontent and the dilemma of how to deal with privilege in the face of others' dispossession. Intimate, well-observed dialogue and complex characterisation show a deeply perceptive mind at work and her plays embrace a variety of different styles, from the moments of expressionism in *My Heart's a Suitcase* (Royal Court Theatre Downstairs, 1990) to the social realism of her most recent play *The Thickness of Skin* (Royal Court Theatre Upstairs, 1996).

Clare's other plays include: *Better A Live Pompey Than A Dead Cyril* (an adaptation of the poems and writings of Stevie Smith for the Women's Playhouse Trust in 1980, for which she collaborated with musician Stephanie Nunn); *I've Been Running* (Old Red Lion, 1986); and *Low Level Panic* (Royal Court Theatre Upstairs, 1988). Her radio work includes: *I've Been Running* (BBC Radio 4, 1987); *Walls of Silence* (BBC Radio 5, 1994); and *The Art of Sitting* (BBC Radio 4, 1996). She has received numerous awards for her work, including the Beckett Award in 1989 and the *Evening Standard* and London Drama Critics' Most Promising Playwright Awards in 1990 for *My Heart's a Suitcase*. *My Heart's a Suitcase* and *Low Level Panic* are published in one volume by Nick Hern Books, who also publish a single edition of *The Thickness of Skin*.

* * *

You've worked a lot as an actress – what made you want to write plays?

I was modestly, averagely successful as an actress. I had time on my hands. In the Women's Theatre Group I did a compilation of Stevie Smith's poetry and prose and that was a very formative experience. It was a step towards playwriting. I was very keen that all the words in the piece were Stevie Smith's and I put them together into a sort of collage. I created Stevie Smith-type characters. So that was the first thing. The Women's Theatre Group was a tremendous time because it was very confidence-building. I could come in with that sort of suggestion and it would be taken seriously. *Better A Live Pompey Than A Dead Cyril* was created alongside the rest of the company's projects and I worked with a musician, Stephanie Nunn, who wrote wonderful music for it. We basically came up with this show and took it on the road and we all earned money for fifty-two weeks of the year! They were halcyon days really. And there were things I wanted to say. I think it must be what drives anybody to write. But writing a new play is a colossal task.

Do you think your work as an actress has helped to make you a better playwright? Perhaps given you a different approach from playwrights who haven't performed?
Oh totally. I act everything as I'm going along. I do this all the time. I can't imagine not having that voice in my head. I have a whale of a time with speeches, like the one Laura has about 'want' in *The Thickness of Skin*. As an actress, you're on top of the material. No, that sounds pretentious. You're not on top of it, you're inside it. Maybe that sounds more pretentious!

How supportive was the theatre industry when you made the switch from actress to playwright? Did you come up against any difficulties?
I met with encouragement, but it takes me ages just to come up with things. It's not like I'm knocking on the door every six months to say, 'Here's another play.' It takes me a long time. It also takes people a long time to commit because it's a big investment putting somebody's play on, which is something you don't sort of realise. I remember with *Low Level Panic*, I learnt afterwards, or during it, that it was costing thirty or something thousand pounds. I thought, 'Blimey, that's my little play.' I've actually met with tremendous support.

Some of your characters, like Jo and Celia in *Low Level Panic* and even Laura in *The Thickness of Skin* are victims in one way

or another. Do you ever worry that when you portray women like this you are reinforcing negative images?

I think Laura's very moving and engaging because she is very genuinely trying hard. The play makes her confront her own behaviour and motivation. If she was perfect she'd be tedious and you wouldn't have a play and she wouldn't have Eddie in her flat. She wouldn't be screwed up about sex and having relationships and she wouldn't be secretive and devious. That's more interesting. And I think Mary in *Low Level Panic* is really tough and that's what I wanted to say in the play. She was assaulted and she's saying 'I'm going to take charge of this.' Some people don't get that. I've had people saying, 'But she spoils her dress! She completely spoils it!' Yes. That's the point. She's a very angry person, but I also think she's great. The play is meant to be humorous and I have seen it done when it's incredibly unfunny. Humour is very difficult to harness. Nobody's without fault or flaw or vulnerability and that's what makes people interesting.

How did the idea for *Low Level Panic* come about?

The plays evolve. I didn't set out to write a play with three women talking intimately in a bathroom. As the material emerged that emerged also, and the title. The assault was something that had happened to me and that was a key thing. I don't remember how I put the thing together. I read a lot of books. I read Andrea Dworkin, Betty Frieda and that extraordinary *My Secret Garden* by Nancy Friday. I read that sort of material, and for the bits of pornography at the beginning that I was trying to write, I bought magazines. Then I doctored bits from those with my own words. That stuff about 'She had an orgasm every time he pushed it in and every time he pulled it out' came directly out of reading pornography. That's straight out of a magazine and people read this! The thing that's very rewarding is when you've written something and you go and see it performed and the audience engages with it and they're full of it and want to talk about it and it's obviously making them think. That's marvellous. The things I've written about are the things that concern me and I'm working out my concerns, I suppose. It's marvellous when you get that reward; that it matters in a similar way to other people. It goes back to, do you have a responsibility? Yes, of course you do.

Some of your writing in *Low Level Panic*, particularly Jo's earlier speeches about her fantasies of herself as the male ideal, must have made some of the men in the audience complicit in the

whole pornography/ideal woman debate. Was that your intention?

No. It was just so stupid. In the original production Caroline Quentin was Jo and everything she did was hilarious because she's a very gifted comic actress: when she was doing her fantasy in the bath it was just so ludicrous, so desperately funny. I've never wanted the play to be without humour. I can't really understand how you can do it without humour, but I have seen it done without and it's a weird play that I feel I have nothing to do with. It's this angst-ridden thing about portraying women as being terminally confused, troubled. It's meant to be funny. If it isn't funny then it's wrong. I mean it's written in such a daft way! When Jo's being sexy, it's just so ludicrous, and she's walking around Mayfair! It's just so ridiculous. That's why the play is set in a bathroom. It is the letting out of the innermost thoughts of humans, allowing them air time. And Mary pulls Jo up all the time and won't join in with this orgy that Jo's going through in her mind. She's not joining in on this fantasy trip and that's why it ends.

When it was first done it was deadly funny to both sexes. The feedback I got from men was tremendous and they didn't feel they had been voyeurs. Celia, who makes it with a bloke, is the closest to that, but she never reveals anything and the other two are in various types of mess. I very much wanted it to be a shabby, towelling dressing-gown club. I went to see a production of the show abroad and it was like a Janet Raeger show and then I thought, 'I have no control over this. I completely loathe this. This is not in any way what it's meant to be and I don't feel that's what I've written, but I can't stop people doing it.' When it was originally done, when Nancy Meckler did it, you felt for those young women. They weren't displaying themselves at all.

My Heart's a Suitcase **weaves symbolism into realism in a very interesting way. Where did Luggage and Pest come from?**

They both sort of emerged. I wanted Chris to have something that she was finding hard to get away from, something that wouldn't let her go, something that was bringing her back to the state that she is in over that weekend, which is like a bad memory she can't get shot of. It's like wanting to get the record straight. She wants to say something about 'Yes, but it does mean something. How do you know what it meant? How do you know what it was doing to me?' It's one of those maddening things that you can't get sorted. You've got to let it go. Chris has this problem: she can't let it go, that's her problem. And it keeps coming back on her when she's at

her lowest ebb. Luggage was dramatic licence really. I thought of
the Patron Saint of Heavy Burdens. It was the symbol for the play
because everybody in that play was carting stuff about with them.
I made her up entirely.

**One criticism that is sometimes made of your work is that you
raise critical social questions, but don't go far enough in
exploring and resolving these. It seems ridiculous to expect playwrights to resolve everything, but do you think this is a fair
criticism?**
I'm not writing a thesis. It's thought-provoking, but it's not a
debate. I like to have people wanting to talk about it. I believe you
can't do better than that. How on earth could I be conclusive in
My Heart's a Suitcase? What, Luggage comes on and gives a finale?
Playwrights are not politicians. That's exactly what they're not.
And with *The Thickness of Skin* I didn't want anyone to be culpable
and it to be that simple.

**Chris's dilemma in *My Heart's a Suitcase* seems to be the dilemma
of any woman who at thirty has chosen not to marry, have
children and conform in the way that society expects her to. Is
that how you saw her?**
The starting point for Chris is, 'I'm thirty and I'm still a waitress.'
All that stuff she says: 'I didn't realise that the choices I made were
choices. I didn't realise these were decisions.' She's very unclear of
how to effect change in her own life and she's not a heroine, you
know, because we aren't. You can talk to women who are my age
and have got a fifteen-year-old and an eighteen-year-old and they're
thinking, 'Well, that's what I did.' But did you choose to do that?
Choice is my big thing. What is it? Do we have it?

**Reviews for *The Thickness of Skin* were almost unanimously
good, but one reviewer did comment that the play came across
as 'one of the most right-wing pieces of theatre' he had ever
seen. Do you feel that the play's tragedy was perhaps misunderstood? That some of the humour let the audience off the hook?**
Isn't it possible to get to people through comedy? I would hope
so. It was humorous and some of the humour was coming out of
recognition, empathy. And if there's laughter at the character
of Imogen, that's uncomfortable and embarrassed. These things are
part of the experience of seeing a play. The play wouldn't be funny
if it was pointing the finger. The play wouldn't engage you if it
was pointing the finger and being accusatory and giving you a

lecture and a blueprint of how things ought to be different. I suppose the starting point was my own sense of muddle about what sort of contribution I make. What's the point of being a nice person and what does that mean? I've heard people, I've talked to people who have said that the play leads straight into conversations about what you give and who you give to.

Were you calling for more government intervention and responsibility?
Well, it does seem to me that a lot has been left to chance, which is insufficient and not workable, and with tragic consequences. Imogen's situation is an extremely difficult one to get right because she wants independent living. She's an adult woman. She wants to be treated with due respect and allowed to live as she wants to live. But the way she wants to live is destroying her, so she needs constant overseeing. I wouldn't want to live next door to her and I'm not the saint who's looking after her. And with Eddie I didn't want him to be a homeless person to provoke a 'Oh, let's all feel terribly sad'. He's complicated in a lot of ways and not very nice.

Like many women dramatists, you have had several successes Upstairs at the Royal Court. Were you disappointed that _The Thickness of Skin_ wasn't given a Downstairs treatment?
Well I think _The Thickness of Skin_ should have been Downstairs. It took me a long time to write and it became an outstanding commission from the Royal Court. I was fulfilling a debt. Yes, it should have been Downstairs. But I don't think, in my experience, women are treated differently. You're in the hands of the people who at the time are making the decisions and you have to be what they want at the time of those decisions. I don't think my play was that fashionable. I get likened to David Hare and that isn't vogue at the moment. The task is a deadly one if you're managing theatres, you know, how to make the right decision. I think women are given fair treatment and I don't think they have to work twice as hard. They are not as numerous. They want to have families and that has an impact upon their lives and their careers that's not accounted for. I personally don't have a family. How many new plays get to be put on the stage anyway? How many new plays happen? The proportion of women who get seen at the Royal Court, I would think, is equal. It has changed a bit, I suppose, since Max [Stafford-Clark] left because he did champion women: Caryl [Churchill], Timberlake [Wertenbaker], me, Sarah [Daniels], Winsome [Pinnock] ... that's a lot. But I wish there were more of

us so that the likelihood, or the chance, of being in the top five as opposed to the next fifteen or the twenty beneath was higher. It's just a process of numbers really.

We need more women dramatists?
Yes. But when you look at it, what's your benchmark? The Lyttelton and the Olivier? New women's work on either stage hasn't happened yet, but what work is out there that should be on those stages? Plays like Caryl Churchill's *The Striker* go on in the Cottesloe. Her play *Mad Forest* could have been on in the Lyttelton. It's just one of those imponderables really. I think it will happen, if there are enough people and they stay doing it long enough, stick with it. I suppose winning awards and things, winning recognition, affirmation, is a stimulus for you to keep going. I don't know how anybody can write plays without any success for years. It's a mug's game.

Pam Gems

Pam Gems is one of our best-known, most celebrated, award-winning and prolific dramatists. She started writing at the age of eight, but first began to have work produced in her early forties, having moved to London from the Isle of Wight with her husband and four children. 'Hungry for theatre', as she says herself, she spent many lunchtimes watching plays on the Fringe while her children were at school. Here she met other women theatre professionals and, in a spirit of mutual support, energy and commitment, her career as a playwright was launched. She has been heralded as a 'feminist icon', a label which she dismisses, but her work has been hugely instrumental in giving women voice and power within the theatre. More recently she has received wide acclaim for her extraordinary biographical plays: *Queen Christina* (Royal Shakespeare Company, 1977); *Piaf* (RSC's The Other Place, 1978, West End and Broadway, with a major revival in 1993 starring Elaine Paige and directed by Sir Peter Hall, which toured nationally before playing a six-month run in the West End); *Camille* (RSC's The Other Place, 1984 and West End); *Stanley* (Royal National Theatre's Cottesloe, 1996 and Broadway, which won the Laurence Olivier Award for Best Play in 1997); and *Marlene* (national tour and West End, 1996–97). Her other plays include the feminist classic, *Dusa, Fish, Stas and Vi* (Hampstead Theatre, 1976 and West End); and *Deborah's Daughter* (Library Theatre, Manchester, 1994). Her adaptations include: *The Blue Angel* (RSC and West End); *The Cherry Orchard* (West End); *A Doll's House* (Tynewear Theatre, Newcastle); *Uncle Vanya* (national tour with Renaissance Theatre Company, then produced at the Royal National Theatre); *Ghosts* (Sherman Theatre, Cardiff, and national tour); and *The Seagull* (Royal National Theatre).

Piaf, *Camille* and *Loving Women* appear in a single Penguin volume; *Deborah's Daughter*, *Stanley*, *Uncle Vanya* and *The Seagull* are all published by Nick Hern Books; *Dusa, Fish, Stas and Vi* is published by Samuel French and in Methuen's PLAYS BY WOMEN VOL. 1; *Queen Christina* in Methuen's PLAYS BY WOMEN VOL. 5, and *The Cherry Orchard* is published by Cambridge University Press. She has also written two novels: *Mrs Frampton* and *Bon Voyage*,

Mrs Frampton which are published by Bloomsbury and is currently working on a screenplay of *Stanley* and several new stage plays including *Natalia, The Snow Palace* and a biographical play about the life of Garibaldi.

* * *

Although you started writing at an early age, you didn't get your plays produced until you were in your forties. Has this had an effect on your work?
Well, it's been both good and bad. The bad thing is that starting so late I'm still schlepping away in my seventies, trying to make it. I'm where I would normally be if I'd started in my twenties, as most do, except that I'm not in my fifties. So I have a problem with physical energy and stress, which gets worse as you get older because your nervous system packs up. The good thing is that if you've done a lot of living before you start to write you have something to write about. I do find a lot of work by young people, though it's often full of energy, inauthentic. I find that a big problem, especially with the more privileged, who tend to be the ones who are successful, who go to university and then become playwrights. As far as I'm concerned they have nothing to tell me at all, because they haven't lived.

You wrote *Dusa, Fish, Stas and Vi* during the seventies, when feminism was relatively new and seeking definition. In the play you explore the difficulties of becoming empowered and equal and each of the characters embodies a different struggle. What was your creative process behind the play?
I don't have an intellectual kick-off, as it were. I don't think writing works like that. It has a mysterious side. I mean we all have a civic side, things that we feel are important politically or socially, and you join groups or write to the press or whatever. Where writing is concerned, it starts from the thalamus rather than the cortex, if you like. The reason I wrote *Dusa, Fish, Stas and Vi* is that I was living in a big house with a whole lot of people. There was a six-piece band in the basement, with all their girlfriends and hangers-on. I was in touch with a lot of young people, so the four characters were very much based on them. It was written for a practical reason, to give parts to women and to use the out-of-work people around. You bring all those very practical elements together and you're not really aware of the subtext. At the time of doing it, you're simply trying to get people on and off stage, trying to get variety and good one-liners. It's such a practical craft. The intellectualis-ation comes when they ask you to write the programme notes. But

1975, when I wrote the play, was also a bad year because Buzz Goodbody [the pioneering RSC director] had died. The play was a lament really.

What's your work process when you are writing?
Well, I'm a very slow starter. I'm not very good in the mornings, but after about eleven I can't wait to get in there. I used to work all day. I can't do that now, because I find typing gets me in the neck, to the point where I'm now trying to use a dictaphone. It's a funny process writing plays because you're stopped at every point by practical problems. It's difficult because you can't learn to write plays without having plays on. It's a far greater problem for women writers, because women still don't have access to the pub and club coterie that men do. Trying to get your first play on, you know ... I like to think it's a little easier, but in fact I don't think it is, because there's been this dread word 'post-feminism', whatever that is supposed to mean.

I watched the film *Shallow Grave* last night, which I had never seen before and I admitted to myself that Danny Boyle had done a good, Tarantino-style job, but in the end I thought, 'Christ, this amorality is getting too much. It's getting luscious and it'll do us in.' If you don't have substance to feed on, very bad things happen. And there's been a total slide in behaviour, with people not caring, not bothering. Art is important. A healthy society is a society that's in tune, at a very deep level, with its own art and artists. If you lose that and if you take people away from their spirituality, their imagination, the deep wells of themselves, things end up in a very bad way. You get this sullen, disaffected, cynical, impoverished society which is ultimately full of rage, which is where we are now, I think. There's no meaning. It's what Jean-Paul Sartre was on about.

You have been celebrated by many as a feminist icon. How easily do this label and this responsibility sit with you?
It doesn't at all, partly because I agree with Brecht that happy is the land that needs no heroes. I am very suspicious of people who set themselves up or find themselves in the position where they feel they have to speak for other people. I believe in the individuality of choice and responsibility. I hate the word icon because what it means is you let go of your responsibility and let somebody else choose for you, which is very dangerous. There are people I admire like Germaine [Greer]. Hers is an unusual mind and she sets the cat among the pigeons, but I don't want her to be my icon. I want

her to be a wacky lady, who makes me laugh and makes me think. Once you get hierarchy, you get passivity. It lets you off the hook, in terms of making your own decisions.

I'm hoping political plays will come back in the political year of an election. I think it's time. I know you have to have leaders in as much as you have to have somebody to run the exchequer or domestic affairs, but look what happens to them. They start believing in their own myth, like Thatcher. They all go that way. Doctors who look after Prime Ministers say that it's only a matter of time before they go barking. This is what I have against the Royal Family. How can they be normal human beings? And if they're not normal human beings, who do they represent? I believe in group activity and group responsibility.

Mary Remnant has said of you that 'Gems is at her best when snatching back the truth about women's lives out of the jaws of a male-constructed history'. Many of your plays have done just this and deconstructed popular fantasies about famous women, reassessing the reality behind the fairytales. How important is it for this sort of re-examination to take place in a public forum such as the theatre?

It's extremely important. It used to be fashionable to say in the seventies that theatre changed nothing, art changed nothing. Auden said it earlier about poetry. It's not true, I don't believe it. We change all the time. We modify all the time, otherwise people wouldn't spend vast sums on advertising. And the second half of this century has been incredibly important. It's the time when women became chemically mutated, which is to say, the Pill came in. Women were finally let out of the harem. We were educated. We got the vote and we became, in the same way as men, existential. We gained the power not to be pregnant every month and instead were able to decide when or if. We're in a time of incredible psychic change and we have a lot of exploration to do. For the first time in mammalian history we've got the chance to be fully paid-up members and we have to find out exactly who we are. It's not a question of their allowing us in. It's a question of our saying, 'This is who we are. This is what our relevant contribution will be. This is how society needs to be amended.' There's so much to look into and that's why we need plays, especially written by women, exploring those big questions: 'What do we want? What can we do without?' And it seems an obvious thing to me if you're writing as a woman, that you want to explode some of the grosser myths that have been erected by men; the sentimentalisation of

women and therefore the reduction of them. It's often a power and
control thing. Reparation is needed. It's also a question of truth. If
art isn't truth, what is it? And there are such gross untruths at the
moment.

**Your women characters were described by one reviewer as
'victim-heroines'. What fascinates you about the dialectic of
women who are strong and talented, but sometimes victims at
the same time?**

I took a lot of flak for *Dusa, Fish*. It was regarded by some people
as depressing because the woman kills herself at the end and is
therefore seen to be a victim and not politically correct; that is a
survivor, a fighter. But my answer would be, 'It's not my job to do
propaganda. It's my job to reflect a situation.' The plays are all
different. It's hard for me personally to lump them together, though
I think I do have a depressive side, which is personal, which is due
to early bereavement and that does tend to crop up. I would regard
Piaf as a survivor. Camille, no, but then what I did to that material
was to make it a threnody to love. They wanted to give love to
each other, not sell it to each other, and society wouldn't allow
that. So they were both victims. He's left as a cold automaton. I
like that play very much. I wish they'd do it again. I don't know
if people saw what I was up to.

With Hilda, in *Stanley*, I'm tied by the fact that it's history. She
did die early. Who can say in actuality that she wouldn't have died
prematurely of cancer if they had not had those traumas, but on
the other hand, their relationship did survive spiritually. They were
both damaged. They were all victims, Dorothy Hepworth as well,
and Patricia Preece, because she really did have an artistic talent,
but she didn't do anything with it. Drama itself doesn't deal with
things going right. Drama comes from collision, problems, crisis.
When we know what our solution should be, then our job as
citizens is to implement it. That, for me, is not drama. That's when
I want my money back.

***Queen Christina* was rejected by the Royal Court on the grounds
that 'it appealed more to women than men'. Do you think we
are any further down the road in terms of plays by women and
plays with women protagonists being accepted as readily as their
male counterparts, as worthy of speaking on behalf of human-
kind and the universal?**

No, I don't think we're any further. In a way I think we've slipped
back. We've had all those years of conservatism. The Royal Court

is doing some interesting new work, though not much by women.
It's mostly all this pseudo-butch stuff: the alienated urban creature
– doing what America did ten years ago. All they want is to be
Quentin Tarantino or Bruce Willis, you know? That's what their
aim is. And I find it's the same with all these male directors in
theatre. They want to be movie directors. And where are the great
female roles? Emily Lloyd maybe, seven years ago in one film where
she was this wacky sixteen-year-old protagonist. Kay Mellor's *Band
of Gold* had some lovely roles for women. She cut out myriads of
reality about women surviving, about women around the world
and prostitution. But in the theatre, I can't think of anything where
there was a really sparky, female protagonist.

And on television you mostly get these awful, sentimentalised
things. Television is important after all, because it's what most
people watch. It's where the icons and the models tend to be
revealed. You had silly models like the Penelope Keith type for a
while, gently mocking, but at the same time people found her
reassuring; that nice, safe, suburban pseudo-person. But there's very
little of complexity, where a woman is allowed to be an unpredict-
able human being, or to take the lead. And when she does, she's
the woman doctor. I don't know why that grates on me, but it
does. It's the inaccuracy.

Do you think that's going to change?
If women really took the centre-ground, then I think we would
start to get more women protagonists. But a lot of women don't
want to. I don't think we have the same competitiveness that men
have. It's not that we don't have the guts for it, or the ability, but
there's not that morbid need to be top dog. Thatcher was an
anomaly. She was like the odd mare steeple-chasing.

**As a playwright you are best known and celebrated for the
biographical plays you write. What attracts you to the life of a
particular individual?**
Most of the biographical plays have been by accident. I was asked
to do *Piaf* for a Romanian actress who couldn't get work and
who'd been singing Piaf songs on the street. I was asked to do
Camille for a festival production. *The Blue Angel* was for the Half
Moon when they were going through a rocky patch, but I refused
to do it unless they got the rights to the book and then Trevor
Nunn happened to read it. The only one I really did by design was
Stanley because I love his paintings very much and I hate the way
that we in England dismiss our own painters. And one of the plays

I'm doing at the moment is about Garibaldi and that's deliberate because he was the first pop hero and he is a hero of mine, because he was an unambitious man and I love him. I think it's quite useful, though, to start with a known protagonist because, in a way, you start one act in. You introduce people to a semi-familiar world and then you play another game. It's a hook to sell the play and to get people in the door and then you play your own game. So it's a trick in a way. It's just as exciting to start with characters you've made up yourself, but it is much harder to sell those plays because producers and managers are buying a pig in a poke and things are so difficult in theatre nowadays.

What sort of research do you do?
I just read everything I can get my hands on, which in the case of *Piaf* was very little. There was one book at the time, written by her putative half-sister. But fortunately, because Piaf didn't die until 1963, I did manage to meet a lot of people who'd known her. And since she lived a café life and had a lot of gay friends, I was able to find out quite a lot, from people who knew her and liked her and loved her and were scorched by her.

How do you decide which bits of information to extract?
You just take what you want. You have a theme; you're simply making use of these people. You see it's not a documentary, it's a play. You're using whoever that person is, who may be a famous person, simply as a weapon for your theme. I'm not at all inhibited by the necessity to keep to the facts. Obviously you mustn't traduce or go against well-known facts to the extent that you're going to alienate or puzzle your audience so much that you lose them. You have to carry them along with you and you do that by what you hope is the poetic truth of what you're saying, so that people will absorb, as you did yourself, the reason for using Stanley Spencer, for example, for an exploration into the nature of marriage. In these so-called post-modernistic times, everything's been in inverted commas and with *Stanley* I took off the inverted commas and I dared to play directly. It's risky, because you're going against fashion, but I couldn't see any other way to do that man. I just wanted to celebrate. One, I had a great feeling for him because he's working class like me. Two, he was brought up between two rivers, as I was, and it gives you a certain vagueness of spirit. And then, you know, this whole problem for the artist which is the difference between the total truth that's necessary for art and the total lack of truth that's necessary for living, which was his problem. That awful

innocence which was so destructive. I love that about him. It's dramatic. He just had bad luck falling into the hands of this very maudite girl, Patricia. I'd like to have explored her more. There's a play there, about such a woman.

In your biographical plays particularly, you often use a non-naturalistic device whereby your characters simply step from one time or scene to another. Do you use this device because you need to include so many events?
I've been very influenced by film, the techniques I use are filmic: the short scenes, jump cuts. And one of the reasons is that people are much more sophisticated. I've done a lot of translation work, or rather adaptation – because I don't speak Russian or Norwegian. When you get the literal translation it's all spelled out. If it's Ibsen, it's a lot wittier and funnier than people think. It's not the ploddy stuff that you usually see, but he does spell everything out, 'So you came back and then you came to this house and you sat here and I sat there and after a while you said to me . . .' He had to spell it out, but we've had seventy years of cinema language and people learn. In the old days of filming you had to see someone get in the car, drive the car and get back out. Now you jump cut. So we can use that in theatre. And it's not doing Ibsen down by having someone come in and say, 'I don't want to be here anymore.' One line instead of forty-five lines. 'I've had enough,' that's all you need to say now to encapsulate the same thing.

It has quite an emotional impact as well. There's a scene in *Stanley* where Patricia and Stanley are almost having sex as you see Hilda, simultaneously, getting more and more ill. It makes a powerful statement in itself.
Yes. It's very emblematic. Marriages and relationships are so unstable nowadays. There's so much pain and misery around. It's all a bit pre-conscious, you know, writing. You have to really go into that dream and record what that dream is. A lot depends on your own boredom threshold. I have a very low boredom threshold and I just kick on when it bores me. I think, 'Throw it out,' until I engage and amuse myself again. And you just hope that it will engage other people.

Your work is quite subversive. How important is this to you?
Well, I think theatre is by its nature subversive and words are better than guns. I think it's quite a painless way to change people's minds. It's entertainment. You're getting a fair deal. I laugh when people

call us luvvies, because I think to myself, 'Aha! You don't realise you're being got at.' It doesn't always work, of course, but I think you can show people a mirror and make them aware. If you feel passionately about something, and in the end that's the only reason to write a play, you are trying to persuade people to a different point of view; to be bolder, to want to make changes in their lives, or whatever your theme is. And you do that not by saying, 'Don't be so isolationist,' but by showing an isolationist and by showing that he's an absolute prat. In that way, you can persuade people without hurting feelings and, occasionally, that's what drama does.

I think a good piece of theatre often works quite quietly. The main thing is that you come out feeling nourished. You've had food, perhaps just the feeling that you are important as a human being, that what you're feeling matters. We're getting so zombified; you pick up the bloody phone and there's some machine answering it. You should come out of the theatre feeling stronger, warmer, kinder, nicer and more belligerent if necessary, depending on the play. It's when nothing happens that it's so disappointing.

Since the beginning of your playwriting career you have witnessed the near death of the Fringe. What do you think this will mean, and has already meant, in terms of new writing, experimentation and freedom of expression?
I think it's been disastrous because you cannot learn to write plays without actually putting your plays onto a stage. Playreadings are better than nothing, but they're no good really because you've got to have actors and actresses on the floor doing it. It's the only way you learn and we've been denied that. Horrible, ominous things have happened like denying grants so that only middle-class kids are able to go to drama school. It's going to be like it used to be. It is totally disastrous and I'm pinning my hopes on the new government. I really honour the people who have hung on, like the Soho Poly, the Bush, BAC and the other pub theatres. They are heroes and heroines. They don't make a buck, yet they go on doing play festivals and new writing. But it's hell. You're scraping by all the time, cap in hand. And we don't have enough patrons. But so often what you see on the Fringe has *life*. It might be formless, there might be a couple of bad performances, but it has life.

At the National Theatre's Glass Ceiling conference recently, you referred to the dearth of plays by women being produced as 'a gross misrepresentation of half the population'. Can you tell us

more about your feelings on this and how you think we can best fight for change?

Well, it does seem anomalous that statistically more women go to the theatre than men and yet women seem to have so little power over what they see and over what is chosen on their behalf. As to how to rectify this, I think the only way is for women in the theatre – actors, designers, directors, administrators – to get together. We need places to meet, and groups. In the end it comes down to energy, but it's difficult when things are hard anyway and you have very little money and you're out of work, to get up the energy to be dashing around the manor, yet it's the only way.

I often think the theatre world is like the criminal world. I remember talking to a criminal once and he said, 'The trouble is, you can't pick up a phone and take an order. You've got to get out there, fucking keep going after people and you never know where you are.' And I thought. 'Just like the theatre.' There's this kind of hierarchy, an inner circle, which really annoys me. It's horrible, but you have to wait to be picked, unless you get together and form your own power-base. Then you get respect. It may be grudging, but you get respect.

Jenny McLeod

Jenny McLeod, as she says herself, simply loves writing, and, fuelled by her passion, she has produced a significant amount of work in different media over the last ten years. She began writing plays in the middle of her A-levels when she saw an advertisement in a local newspaper in Nottingham (where she grew up) and thought, 'Well, why not do that?' She quickly became hooked, on discovering that it was 'the best buzz I'd ever had'. Encouraged by winning Writing 87 at the Nottingham Playhouse with *Cricket at Camp David*, she went on to write *Island Life* for Monstrous Regiment (produced at Nottingham in 1988 and at the Drill Hall in 1989, before touring nationally). Her other plays include: *The Mango Tree* (for Strange Fruit Theatre Company, which toured nationally in 1990); *The Wild At Heart Club* (for the National Youth Theatre, 1994); *Raising Fires* for the Bush Theatre (also in 1994); and *Victor and the Ladies*, which was produced at the Tricycle Theatre in 1995. She was Writer-in-Residence at the Nottingham Playhouse between 1991 and 1992 and, after winning a Thames Television bursary, had a resident dramatist attachment at the Tricycle Theatre in 1995, during which time her youth play, *It's You!*, was also produced.

Her television work includes *The Wake*, which was screened by BBC Pebble Mill in 1990 and is published as part of the BBC Books series, *Debut on 2*. *Island Life* is published by Nick Hern Books in MONSTROUS REGIMENT – A COLLECTIVE CELEBRATION. Jenny has led a number of creative writing workshops at the Royal Shakespeare Company, Nottingham Playhouse, Derby Playhouse and the Tricycle Theatre. She is currently completing a new screenplay, *Molly and the Outlaws* and a novel entitled *Stuck Up a Tree* for Virago/Little Brown.

* * *

You first started writing plays at a very young age, when you were halfway through your A-levels, and you hadn't really had a theatre background. What made you turn to playwriting?

Well, I just started writing really. It wasn't necessarily that I started writing plays. I wrote a novel first and then poems. I saw an advert to write a play for a competition and that started it all off. I thought, 'I can do that.' I was young and naive. I tried it and spent the next four years revising this play, *Cricket at Camp David*, and sending it out. I took a look at what people said, reworked it accordingly and then I sent it to Nottingham Playhouse and it won the competition there.

How important do you think competitions are for giving writers exposure and getting their work noticed?
I think they are very important. It's a cheap and easy way for new writers to get into the theatre, because it's so difficult, especially with a new play and a new name. Already under-funded companies have to have a lot of faith in any writer they put on, never mind one that no one has ever heard of before. The gamble is so huge for most theatre companies that they just won't pick up an unsolicited script from an unknown and say, 'Yes, we're going to do it. We're going to commit to it.' Competitions are a good way of bringing an unknown into the workings of a theatre. There aren't enough of them available to the first-time writer and there should be. A competition is also how I got my TV break.

You have been very clear about the fact that as a writer you want to be free to explore anything which interests you, that you don't want to 'bang drums', or write 'from a black perspective' or get 'bogged down writing about things that only affect women'. Why is this so important to you?
To begin with that was true, but now my point of view has changed slightly, in that there are so very few black roles for women or black actors. I've also become much more culturally aware of who I am and where I fit into a society like this, where I'm constantly judged. I've become more aware that I'm a black woman living in England since I moved from Nottingham to London three years ago. Things just stand out much more down here. It's more heightened and you'd have to be deaf, blind and dumb not to notice any of it. All this has altered what I said all those years ago. Black and female is some of who I am and I want to explore it. I enjoy writing about my childhood and the things that I know, whereas before, I was afraid to be pigeon-holed. I just wanted to be a writer. But by definition I'm not just a writer. I'm a black woman as well, so that influences my work.

Have you encountered any difficulties in the theatre world as a result of being a black, woman playwright?
I think it's helped, actually. A lot of theatres want to be seen as being very liberal and 'right on'. The business traditionally is quite liberal anyway, but a lot of them want to be seen to employ a black, woman writer. It goes in my favour. And I'll exploit it fully!

In *Island Life* you explore the lives of three old women and something that comes out of the play is the need for them to cling to their pasts and to illusory fantasies. Do you think this happens because our society isolates and abandons old people? Is it something you thought about?
Not while I was writing it, no. I tend to think whatever people get from a play, they get from it. It doesn't mean that I consciously put it there. I'm not saying that's not in the play, but I didn't sit down and say, 'Now this is what I'm going to write about.' I haven't got plays stored in my mind about themes I want to explore. What I did like about *Island Life* was the way the characters all colluded to differing degrees in the illusions and fantasies. It's like they all existed in this fragile world and they all understood how that world worked. They understood that it would only take one of them to step out of that world and it would all come crashing down around them. People live like that. They can convince themselves of anything if it eases whatever pain it is they're nursing. We all do it.

Emmy seems subservient to Sofia, addressing her as 'Miss Sofia' throughout the play, though she also acts as the conciliator. Why did you choose to characterise her in this way?
I liked the idea of Emmy *appearing* subservient to these two slightly mad white women, but in many ways Emmy was the one who held what my mum calls 'the whip hand'. She knows more about what's going on and the way they all fit together than either Vera or Sofia.

You once said about creating your characters that you don't 'put words in their mouths'; they put words on your paper. Is writing still such a spontaneous experience for you?
I try to let it be. But with deadlines and all the things I've been doing this year, it's quite difficult to still write from that point of view. But I understand that if it's going to be good, then that's what happens. There's no point sitting there and saying, 'You'll say this and you'll do this,' because it just doesn't work.

For your play *Raising Fires* you chose the historical setting of Essex in 1603. Why did you want to focus on this era?

I wanted a situation where there was only one black character and I wanted it to be a situation where she was isolated. To go back in time seemed the logical thing. Plus I wanted to explore this whole thing about witches and fires, so 1603 fitted naturally. I remember seeing *The Crucible* when I was at school, and when I was in the middle of the first draft of *Raising Fires*, I read it again. The idea of the witches came from that and also black people's situation in history. That interested me greatly. When I talk to my white friends about what it's like for me walking around the streets of London, it's a complete shock to them. They just don't understand how things work if you're black. *Raising Fires* looks at all that. Tilda's father had no idea of the effect that bringing her to 1603 Essex would have on her. He just thought he was rescuing a little, black, orphan child and that's as far as it went. Witches were scapegoated in much the same way as black people in this society. We're blamed for unemployment, lack of decent housing and the crime rate! It was just a brilliant metaphor for that. We're accused of everything that can go wrong. You know, there's only one black woman in the entire village and it's because of her that things happen!

Did you also want to explore the politics of difference and how difficult it is for an outsider to be accepted and trusted in a society to which they are not necessarily indigenous?

Yes, definitely. Sometimes I like to think that Tilda could have been black or white, it was just her innocence that people leapt on. She was just someone different, naive and different. People are not accepted. I was born here. You go to certain parts of England and it's like you're visiting from outer space. Even where I live, I went into a shop and I was looking for the *Guardian*, but they'd run out, so I walked out and didn't buy anything and I could see the manager watching me out of the corner of his eye, to see if I'd taken anything from his shop. A high number of times that happens because I'm black. It doesn't matter what you do or how well you do it, some people only see one thing when they see you, which in itself isn't a bad thing, but if they've already formed opinions about you because of the first thing they see, then how easy is it going to be to live in a society like this? It's the witch element again. When people get scared about their position in society, they look for the difference around them. It's not white nature. It's human nature.

You have written three youth plays, including *The Wild At Heart Club*. Why is your involvement with young people so important to you?
It isn't that important to me. They were opportunities that just came up. It's not something that particularly interested me.

You're a good, jobbing writer, aren't you?
Yes, I am. You can be really precious about this and come up with all kinds of theories, but I'm not. It's my job. It's what I do. I tailor characters to situations, or opportunities that I get offered. I hate opportunities to pass by because you never know when they're going to come back. And I don't think that's anything to be ashamed of. It's the way I've always done it. Other writers have burning ideas that they want to explore and if it works for them, fine. I feel compelled to write, but not about anything in particular.

Do you think about the way you're going to tell a story before you sit down to write it?
It's just where the character leads you. If I put too much structure or form on it too early, then it doesn't work. It doesn't interest me, and if I'm not interested, I get bored. I try to have some idea of where the story might go, but it's very loose. Things change all the time.

When you go into rehearsal do you find it exciting seeing your work come to life?
I actually hate rehearsals, to tell you the truth. With *Victor and the Ladies*, because Paulette Randall directed it, and we got to be good friends, I said to her, 'I'll be there for the read-through and once you've gone through the play and we've gone through queries from the actors, then I'm going.' I feel as if I've done my job and now it's their turn to do their job. Playwriting is a process where you pass it on. I leave the ring, basically. And also it's quite painful, sitting there watching someone trying to understand what you've written and pulling it apart, to make it fit together the way they need it to. I don't like being around for that. And you have to let go because you're not a director. If you want to direct, go and direct, but you can't do it from the writer's chair. But it's still brilliant to see them bring the characters to life; to see them get what you intended, and more.

In *Victor and the Ladies*, Shirley asks 'How has a man like him managed to get all these women?' which is a good question,

since he deceives and disrespects them all constantly. **Did you want to look at why some women allow themselves to be treated so badly?**

Yes. Actually this was the one play where I did sit down and think, 'Yeah, this is the theme I want to explore,' because, I think especially in the black community, this happens a lot. When Paulette and I started talking about the play, we were regaling stories about all the women we knew who were in this situation. For a man to have four women is not unusual. And the story of Victor not knowing which woman to marry, I know the woman that that's based on.

Victor comes out as the weakest character in the play and the women, though they have their personal weaknesses, are strong, especially when they are united as a sisterhood. Did you intend the message of the play to be feminist?

Not consciously. Having said what I said about me wanting to explore certain themes within this play, I didn't sit down and arm-wrestle the play into being. For me it's just a play about a group of strong women who know what they want. My mother and all the women I grew up around were strong. They had to be. The men I knew never quite had the strength of the women. They never needed it in ways that the women did. Women have a different deal in society. It wasn't me taking a stand and making the women in *Victor and the Ladies* stronger. Women have always seemed stronger to me. I've never known it any other way. I was also sending up West Indian males and I enjoyed that totally.

There are some very funny moments in the play, especially the magic ritual with the knickers and toenails, which was very inspired. What gave you the idea?

It's through listening to my mother. I've got four sisters and when we were growing up I spent a lot of time sitting under the kitchen table listening to my mum tell stories about who was having who, who wasn't having who, and also about Obea and magic. She actually knows somebody who used their knickers and toenails in a ritual.

British Theatre is still too biased towards white, middle-class culture. How would you like to see the situation change?

I don't see how it's going to change. Most theatres don't take risks on black playwrights, or on women playwrights. Winsome [Pinnock] and I can write as many plays as we can write, and all of them can get put on, but it's still not enough. There needs to be more. I was lucky. I just didn't believe that I could *not* do it. So I did it. And I've had help. Since I got my break I've had two residencies at the Nottingham Playhouse and at the Tricycle and that has helped me to keep writing and to have a regular wage, which is really difficult to achieve. It's like hanging from a branch every single day, and I can understand why so many people are not attracted to being playwrights, especially being black, female playwrights. I don't know how you get around the fact that there's me and Winsome and one or two others. It's also about being on the outside of this little clique of theatres and thinking, 'Well, they're not going to be interested in anything I've written. It's not going to get past the front door.' There's a lot of talent out there, but people think it's just not worthwhile sending anything in because it's not going to get past the first hurdle.

So if we could put you in charge of changing the British theatre, what would you do?
I think we need to get out of these big, imposing buildings that are so much to do with the past. Some people think that a play belongs simply in a purpose-built auditorium and nowhere else. I think plays belong anywhere where people are. There should be more geared towards touring companies and getting theatre to a different, but an equally important, audience; one that might not go into a building and sit in the dark for two hours, but one that deserves the buzz of a live performance and can't always afford the cost of a night out at the theatre, especially in London.

Bryony Lavery

A champion of gay and lesbian theatre, Bryony Lavery has swum against the mainstream with verve, nerve and success since the beginning of her career in the early seventies. A wizard of humour and theatricality, she has produced a vast array of work, displaying huge range and diversity. A rounded theatre practitioner, her skills extend to: performer (most notably as Tinkerbell in *Peter Pan* at the Drill Hall), artistic director (Gay Sweatshop 1989–91 and Female Trouble), writer of children's theatre (including *The Dragon Wakes*) and of many cabarets (including *Floorshow* with Caryl Churchill for Monstrous Regiment in 1977).

As a playwright her work includes: *The Catering Service* (Edinburgh Festival and tour, 1975); *The Family Album* (ICA and national tour, 1976); *Bag* (Young Vic and two national tours, 1976); *Grandmother's Footsteps* (King's Head Theatre, 1977); *Helen and Her Friends* (King's Head Theatre, 1978); *Missing* (Sheffield Crucible and national tour, 1979); *Hot Time* (Common Stock Theatre Company, 1979); *The Wild Bunch* (Women's Theatre Group tour, 1979–80); *Witchcraze* (Women's Theatre Group tour and Pocket Theatre tour, 1980); *Calamity* (Tricycle Theatre and national tour, 1983); *Origin of the Species* (Birmingham Rep and Drill Hall, 1984 and 1985); *The Two Marias* (Theatre Centre national tour, 1988); *Kitchen Matters* (for Gay Sweatshop, Royal Court and national tour, 1990); *Her Aching Heart* (for Sphinx, two national tours, 1990); *Wicked* (Clean Break Theatre Company, national tour, 1990); *Flight* (Perspectives Theatre Company, Masken Theatre, Denmark, 1991); *Creature* (Perspectives Theatre Company tour, 1992); *Goliath* (Sphinx national tour and the Bush Theatre, 1997); and *More Light* (BT National Connections, 1997).

Bryony's television work includes the BBC comedy series *Revolting Women*. Her radio work includes adaptations of *My Cousin Rachel* and *Wuthering Heights* for BBC Radio 4, and *Laying Ghosts*, *Kindred Spirits*, *Cliffhanger*, *Helen and Her Friends* and *Velma and Therese* also for BBC Radio 4. Her plays are published in HER ACHING HEART AND OTHER PLAYS (Methuen), THE WILD BUNCH AND OTHER PLAYS (Nelson), *Origin of the Species* in PLAYS BY WOMEN

VOL. 6 (Methuen) and *Witchcraze* in HER STORY – THREE PLAYS (Sheffield Academic Press). She has also written a short essay entitled 'Writing with Actors . . . or The Playwright gets out of her Garret' in *Women Writers Handbook* (Aurora Metro Press), a chapter entitled 'But will men like it? Or living as a feminist writer without committing murder' in *Women and Theatre* (Faber & Faber) and two short radio plays for schools, *Uniform and Uniformed* and *Numerical Man* in *Masks and Faces* (Macmillan). She is currently working on two new stage plays: *About Suffering* and *Ophelia*; a book about Tallulah Bankhead; a play for BBC Radio 4, *No Joan of Arc*, and a new television detective series for Channel 4 entitled *Private Dyke*. Bryony also teaches on Birmingham University's MA course in Playwriting.

* * *

You worked with a number of alternative theatre groups such as Gay Sweatshop and Monstrous Regiment in the seventies, when theatre was better funded and more able to experiment and explore important political and sexual issues. You have survived through its demise, yet still managed to retain your humour and hope. How have you achieved this?

I don't know, actually! Being naive, I don't think I noticed that things were as dreadful as they were, because I have worked constantly. I always notice things in retrospect, so I hadn't realised it had changed that much, until it had changed. My sense of humour fortunately stays with me, apart from a few days a year when I think life is miserable and the world is unfair, but that's for a very short time.

So you're still optimistic about what theatre can do? Even though it's much more difficult nowadays to produce work?

Well, is it? With the very first show I took to Edinburgh I don't know how we lived. I mean, we lived in a flat that was virtually a bomb site and we were scraping money together. I wouldn't do that now. I'd be dead if I did that now! And I can remember in the seventies being cross with people who got money when I didn't and when I got money certain people thought it was unfair, so I don't think it's different. I think it's always difficult. If you're doing work which attacks society people don't throw money at you. And if they do, it's very worrying, because why are they? I still subscribe to the jester theory that, you know, the jester had to be funny and provide amusement and when you didn't you got your head knocked off and I'm thinking more and more that that's how it works; either your reputation goes and you get more money or you get less money.

In your play *Kitchen Matters*, there is a lot of anger as well as humour. Was your purpose in writing it to attack the funded mainstream theatre, in the light of the threat of closure of Gay Sweatshop at the time?
Yes. It was actually that. They commissioned me to do the play and I was one of its unpaid artistic directors. The Arts Council had started saying, 'We think it's had its day. We think it should go.' They had all sorts of different and conflicting reasons why there shouldn't be a Gay Sweatshop. I was very angry. We were all very angry that we were being threatened and there didn't seem to be a strong reason for it, because we were still doing very good work. It seemed important that the play came to the centre of that. It was wonderful to write something that was like a knife against them. It was so exciting.

You have never received the mainstream recognition that you deserve for your work. How do you feel about this? (*Bryony Lavery simulates crying.*) And have there ever been times when you became so disillusioned that you wanted to stop writing?
No to the last bit. Not for more than about a week. Ninety-nine per cent of the time I feel fine about it, because most of the mainstream people . . . I'm not overawed by the size of their brains, or their ability to judge what I do. And I know in my heart that it's not a competition. Writing is not a competition. You don't have to be best and win prizes. I don't much mind, as long as people put my plays on. There are an awful lot of disadvantages in being recognised by the mainstream. *Why* I don't receive recognition is more important than that I do. Because what does receiving mainstream recognition mean? That Billington likes you? Wow! Michael Coveney? I get very 'important' recognition from some very unimportant people!

It means you do get seen by a much wider audience.
Well again, I think that needs looking at, because my work needs to be seen in the right way and when I go to somewhere like the National and I'm right at the back, my experience isn't huge and whole. I don't know whether I like those big spaces. I'm much more interested in the absoluteness of the experience, rather than that it's mainstream, or everyone says, 'Get down to the Palladium and see Bryony Lavery.' I don't really care about that. Except when my self-esteem is very low, which isn't very often.

Your plays are often two- or three-handers, with the actors

playing multiple parts. This lends itself naturally to theatricality, but is your decision to use only a small cast essentially one of necessity in poverty?

Yes. I do love difficult constraints and creating something for two or three actors is great, which is why I think the National Theatre of Brent works so well, because you're in there thinking, 'We all know there are only two people, so let's see how they can do the entire civil war.' That's fine until you realise that you're doing it for about the fifteenth or sixteenth time, and then I can get cross with that restraint. That's why I need to do things like *Ophelia*, which again, is so far from the mainstream, but it means that I can do twenty-eight parts and that's exciting. But mostly it works as a very artistic constraint. I remember how visually shocked I was when someone took me to the opera. It started with about forty people coming on. We don't get that spirit. We don't know that that's a possibility in the theatre anymore. And that is really criminal. That is when I do notice the lack of money. Shakespeare is wonderful, and one of the reasons he's wonderful is because you get a big cast. You don't have to do a big battle scene with two people. We do now, unfortunately, think of plays as something that a few people perform, which they're not.

Your work, while dealing with a realistic story and contemporary issues, has elements of the mythic and archetypal about it. Why is this important to you?

I like stories, but I think one of my weaknesses is that I have sometimes been quite cavalier about structure. Having a mythic structure is like having a ghost friend, you know, like an aunty or godmother to the story. I like the way you see a story behind a story. It just makes it richer, I think, and they always seem to link. I must be telling a finite number of stories, and the more I do, the more I spot afterwards that there are similar themes. I've got to find different ways of doing that and myth is one of them.

You frequently use parody in your work to humorously undermine and question genres or institutions which annoy you, and this works very effectively without being didactic. Do you think that's why your work is so accessible and palatable? Because the forms you parody are easily recognisable?

Well, yes, but parody has to be good. It's not worth parodying if it's not as good as the original. You can't copy it in a dismissive way. And I don't think I do that because somewhere in my heart I do acknowledge the strength of the first thing I'm copying. I'm using parody to say, 'You'll recognise this and we'll go further,' rather than, 'I despise this,' and I think that's why it works. That, and I don't always go around parodying things. People often say about *Her Aching Heart*, 'Parodying that lush language!' and it was a while before I admitted that I wasn't parodying it at all. I really like using language like 'My heart is like a basset hound' because it makes me laugh, not because I find romantic fiction's language funny, although sometimes it is, but sometimes it's actually very beautiful and wonderful, in a naive way. In *Kitchen Matters*, everybody I parodied, all those pieces of work, were very important to me. So, you know, kitchen-sink drama, Noël Coward and all that, I just thought, 'Whoopee! I can do all these styles in one piece.' You can be clever in a silly way.

You owed a debt to those traditions?
Yes, because the story was really about saying, 'Wonderful as all these traditions are, they do cut out gay people.' There seemed to be something very nice about doing that, because a lot of actors and actresses are in the closet, so there's a truth about saying that all those traditions can embrace lesbians and gays, as well as lesbian and gay theatre. I was having a double joke. That's another reason, of course, why I'm not mainstream, because a lesbian woman can't be deemed to hold central the hopes and fears of humanity yet. I think Sarah [Daniels] suffers from that. But she's more accepted because of where her work is performed.

You often use very simple devices to great effect; for example, in *Witchcraze*, showing us the change from paganism to Christianity in one scene. How do you create such concise and powerful dramatic images?
I don't know! I think about it, but sometimes you don't know where it comes from. Very often, the simplest is the best. I think I'm quite good at finding the simplicity in complex things. When I get complex, I get bad. Different people have different gazes, but I'm quite good at the links between things that are far away. I'm not always good on minutiae.

Your language is unique and brave in that it is simple, almost childlike in its directness, and very powerful as a result. You frequently also invent language to make points about communication and human interaction. Where does this capacity come from? And is this something you work consciously towards?
What words do I make up?

Hehehehe . . . Frit-frit-frit! In *Witchcraze*. It's really simple, but it touches your heart immediately. You can't respond with your head, you have to respond with something else.

I'm very touched to hear that, with my heart! That is where I work from. When I teach writing, I always say, 'Is this from your heart?' Because very often you get tricky young men who want to be clever, rather than true. All writers invent language. I'm not that interested in inventing naturalistic language, I like to aim for something that hasn't been said. I'm attracted somehow to characters who are dumb, because making them speak seems to me what I'm here for. I know I'm not an intellectual and I'm not an academic, so my characters have to relate to each other, rather than argue, because that's the language I'm more interested in. That's quite interesting, because I'm quite a rageful writer. It's hardly buried at all. In Zen terms, the moment you feel and express your anger absolutely, it vanishes. And I think there's something about the characters trying to find the language to express that anger or that hurt or that love, and they need new words for it. But by the time I've created it, it's there, so I don't feel I've invented it.

And also, because it's not naturalistic, it can't go in one ear and out the other and not be absorbed. It actually jars you, to make you listen, because it's something that you haven't heard before. It gets right into your body.

That may be another reason why I'm not mainstream, because that must be quite uncomfortable. And if it goes there, then people might not have the words to say what's happened. You know, there's a large part of the mainstream that is about being comfortable, and I think there's a certain comfort in cleverness, that if you know why something over there is going wrong, it's much easier to deal with. I get strong reactions, both good and bad. Sometimes I've had people get very hurt and upset.

Do you have to dig deep to get to that truth?

Yes. I think all writers would say that. Virginia Woolf said, 'I'm writing this down, so that I will remember when I'm writing that I feel like this.' The horror of it is thinking that you have nothing to say, or nothing that's new or that it all feels slightly second-hand. There's always a point when that happens and you have to go through that, and then, somehow, across the other side, you're at the point where you want to write. I find that in the network, the secret writing network. You know, Sarah [Daniels] rings me up, or I ring her up, or Olwen Wymark, and they're experiencing the same thing. But somewhere on the other side, once you've got through everything that's been said already, there's a new way of saying almost the same thing, like 'Life's hard'. I think plays are about rehearsing awful or wonderful events and recovering from them.

All your plays are physical and rely heavily on the actors' use of their bodies to create the atmosphere and make a scene, which is quite unusual. Why is this important to you?
Well, what would you rather see? Would you rather see someone sitting there talking or would you rather see them moving around? It's because I'm a very physical writer. I only discovered that when I was writing *Her Aching Heart*, in that when I was writing the modern characters I was like that (*she makes a small, physical gesture*) but when I was writing the historical ones I was almost like that (*she makes a very funny, expansive gesture*). And I suddenly realised that it's because I somehow let them inhabit me physically. I need to know how they move. I haven't enough confidence to be a performer, so I want to release that in my writing. I don't like the notion of an actor sitting in the dressing room for all but five or ten minutes of the play, because they don't like it. All of them want to be on stage for as long as they possibly can, doing as much as they can. I'm really not interested in lazy actors, so I write for the type of actors who want to be there all the time and who want to throw their bodies and hearts into it, who wouldn't be saying, 'Well, how am I going to do this?' but instead are like, 'I've just got this little idea, let me try it.'

Using the bodice-ripper as a form for *Her Aching Heart* allows you to explore the issues of class, gender and stereotyping. Is that why you chose it?
No. I have explored class and gender issues, but I was quite surprised to discover I had. I've always loved romantic fiction and Claire Grove had said, 'Will you write a play for me?' and I said, 'Yes,' and she said, 'When we've got past this one, I've got to do a two-hander on gender,' and we thought, 'Oh no.' Because describing it, you know, no one thinks, 'Whoopee!' And somewhere halfway through the pizza we were eating, she mentioned romantic fiction and we said, 'Aah. We could put them together.' I was honestly just having fun writing it and I was fulfilling the brief. It's such an affectionate look.

All your women characters free each other and instigate change

**when they challenge and support one another. Do you feel this
sort of positive theatrical representation is missing from mainstream theatre?**

Yes, it is. I don't know why because it's such a rich area. I think
there's a huge fear in a lot of people's hearts at the power of women.
Last week I left off halfway through a clown workshop with Slava
Polunin. He had chosen loads of videos of good male clowns and
I said, 'Why aren't there any women?' and he said, 'There are only
three women clowns that work: the Blue Stocking, the Happy
Grandmother and the Aristocratic Lady.' He said, 'Women clowns
can do work which is to do with the past, but not if it's to do with
the future.' Wonderful clown as he is, he's a Russian man and
that's the future he wants. He wants his women and his women
clowns in the places he wants them. *He* wants to make the future.
So I think that's why. In a lot of the mainstream that I don't like,
the future they want is very similar to the past, and actually doesn't
include women being *really* powerful. It's so deep. I come across
it time and time again. An awful lot of men really don't want to
give up power, which, of course, one understands. And a lot of
women don't really understand what they can have.

**Witchcraze is one of your most establishment-threatening plays.
You knock the foundations of Christianity and capitalism and
show how the demonisation of women came about. You also
show women coming into their power. It's amazingly potent.**

The reviews certainly gave it that 'Don't you come near us!'
response. (*She makes a warding-off-evil-spirits gesture.*) The only
way to do that in criticism is to say, 'It's awful. Incompetent.' We
don't have critics in this country who say, 'This frightened me.'
They have to cover it in cleverness. And this is the least academic
medium there is. It's big and nasty and dirty and noisy.

**The Punch and Judy tableau in Witchcraze is all about male
jealousy and powerlessness in the face of women's capacity to
give life. Do you see this as at the root of all misogyny?**

No. Because I don't think it's jealousy, I think it's fear. I think fear
is at the root of every piece of bad behaviour. I don't know why
they're so frightened, except it's the unknown. We are 'other'. With
women, the way of feeling our fear is to understand it. It seems
that that is not the way men cope with their fear. Their way is to
put it out in the distance, to put the barrier up. But nobody ever
admits to it, it's peculiar. I don't know how you address it.

In *Witchcraze*, and in many of your plays, some of the characters betray their women friends and collude in male oppression, usually out of financial necessity. Is this your attack on capitalism?

Yes. It was clearly about that and betrayal is one of the most hurtful things that we experience and I think certain political constructs aid that. But the first thing for me would be the human feeling of betrayal. I work from the emotion outwards, to the politics, rather than the other way.

In *The Origin of the Species* you explore and re-examine the subject of evolution with a contemporary audience. What prompted you to do this? It was a very interesting and different retelling.

I worked with Gillian Hannah and Mary McCusker from Monstrous Regiment and I can't remember if it was their idea or my idea. We had a three-week workshop and did all sorts of exercises to do with evolution and I read a huge amount. I remember the horror, how the fuse of rage was lit. I'd always known that history was biased, but when I discovered that *pre-history* was biased, that knocked me sideways. To assume that because this lion pride works like this, with the male lion in control, that the entire creation of the world is that way as well! It was like a bomb going off in my head.

Did you get quite a strong audience reaction to the play?

No. It was quite popular. I remember Susie Orbach coming out of it, saying, 'It's such a good mothering play.' And it is quite clearly that as well. It's about the Molly character giving birth, in the most peculiar way, to an absolute baby, who then grows up, from being four million years old, to being a woman of our age. It actually got good reviews. I remember a few courting couples coming and when Mary got up in the hairy suit they couldn't handle it, because if you're a courting couple you can't see a play with a hairy woman in it! But that was all. No, because it was about mothering, as well as the huge subject it was, everybody liked it. There was a mummy in it, and an adorable and bright child.

Ophelia is a significant retelling of Shakespeare's *Hamlet*, where the women are put centre-stage and victims are no longer victims. Do you think women need to re-examine and reclaim Shakespeare because of the huge cultural influence he has?

I don't know the answer to that. And I don't know that I put the women back centrally. I think, they're curiously slippery. It was a way in to writing a large play and it was a very specific brief, and so it was like a clever puzzle for me. I think, to go back to what I was saying a little earlier, one of the reasons people do Shakespeare is not only because he's just wonderful, but because it's the only opportunity around to do large, panoramic pieces about important things. So, in a way, I was leaping on his back to do that. And I do find it interesting, trying to go into somebody else's emotional and artistic landscape. I chose *Hamlet* as the starting point because I did it for A-level. I now understand the importance of having a lot of plays by women on the A-level syllabus, because, you know, I was made to study certain things like *Hamlet* and it leapt out of my psyche, because it had been firmly implanted there.

In most of your plays there is a real cry for women to take action and to celebrate their strength and independence, as Portia says in *Ophelia*, 'To ride to do the deeds that must be done!' Is this a call for women, as well as society, to change?
Yes, to have more confidence. It's not a particularly anti-men thing, it's for themselves. Human beings are infinitely more capable than they think they are. It's very noticeable when you do workshops with people how, particularly women, need to be given permission to improve. It would be a fabulous world if we retained that five-year-old 'I can do this. I'm the most wonderful thing on the planet' confidence. You see people handing over their power, their strength and getting tired and getting grey. I think what I would like is to explode the world back into colour!

Tanika Gupta

Tanika Gupta is a bilingual British Bengali and it is this fusion of cultures and languages which gives her plays, though written in English, their unique and stunning, lyrical quality. She started writing plays in 1991 and although she has been very successful in both radio and television, her remarkable British-Asian voice has met with resistance from the theatre establishment, where her work has been dismissed as 'too community-based', despite its powerful, universal appeal. Though two of her stage plays, *Ananda Sananda* and *Voices on the Wind* (about the struggle of the freedom fighters under British rule), have been given rehearsed readings, neither has received a full production. But the tide is now turning. Tanika is currently Writer-in-Residence at the Soho Theatre Company and in May 1997 her most recent play, *Skeleton*, received its first full production there. In September 1997, her stage adaptation of Gita Mehta novel *A River Sutra* opened at the Three Mills Island Studios, Bromley-by-Bow, directed by Indhu Rubasingham and for the first time her future as a theatre playwright looks optimistic.

Tanika's television work includes: *Flight* (an original screenplay for BBC 2's Screen Two); two episodes of *Grange Hill*; and two short films for the BBC, *Bideshi* and *The Rhythm of Raz* (which was nominated for a Children's BAFTA award in 1995). She recently completed an adaptation of Vikram Seth's *A Suitable Boy* for a proposed Channel 4 series. Her radio work includes *Red Orleanders*, *Asha* (finalist in the BBC Young Playwrights Festival, 1991), *The Bounty Hunter*, *Pankhiraj* (nominated for the Commission for Racial Equality, Prix Futura and Sony awards), and adaptations of her stage plays, *Voices on the Wind*, *Ananda Sananda* and *Skeleton* (all for BBC Radio 4). Her work for BBC Radio 5 includes *Badal and His Bike* (nominated for a CRE award) and four episodes of *Kiss Me Quick*. Tanika's publications include *Rebecca and the Neighbours*, and a short story in the Asian Women Writers' Collective anthology FLAMING SPIRITS, published by Virago. Her play *Skeleton*, is published by Faber & Faber in 1997. She is currently working on a new play, *Flesh and Blood*.

* * *

You have written extensively for TV and radio. What made you turn to the staging?

Talawa were inviting new, black women writers to send in stage scripts and *Voices on the Wind* was selected. But it wasn't for production, it was for development. They put me together with a dramaturg, Matthew Lloyd at Hampstead. I'd see him once a week and he'd look at my play and structure it. That was quite interesting, because I didn't really know how to write a play for the stage. All my scenes were really short and characters would say things like, 'I am walking across the room now.' But I think I caused a lot of trouble at Talawa because of that whole thing of their producing black writing and the different definitions of 'black'. I don't think Asian fitted in. But what is the definition of an Asian play? I don't think *Voices on the Wind* is 'Asian'. That whole definition presupposes that only an Asian audience would want to see the play and I don't think that's true. As long as it's a universal story, it should appeal to everyone. *Voices on the Wind* ended up having two performances at the National Theatre Studio. The director, Indhu Rubasingham, was invited there to workshop something for three weeks and to their shock she took me. I think they were expecting her to do a Chekhov or something. They didn't expect her to take a modern, Asian, woman writer. It was quite weird. It was like we'd broken into the National Theatre Studio and we weren't supposed to be there. But they were good to us. They gave us space and we produced *Voices on the Wind* at the end of it and people came to see it.

Has being an Asian woman caused you any problems in making your debut as a playwright in the theatre?

It's been difficult. You get patronised a lot. At the end of *Voices on the Wind* one particular literary manager came up to me and said he loved the play and that he was particularly interested in developing Asian women writers. I was so pissed off. I said to him, 'Look at me. I'm over-developed already.' They want to 'develop' you, and you get to the point where you think, 'Actually, I've written quite a lot now and I'm not exactly a new writer anymore. It's time you actually put our plays on.'

Do you feel that there are no openings for you as an Asian writer?

No, there aren't. Everyone's very concerned with bums on seats.

While literary managers might like my writing, artistic directors don't believe that it's going to bring in the punters. I had the most extraordinary letter from Hampstead Theatre which said something about *Voices on the Wind* being a wonderful play, politically interesting and emotionally exciting, but that at the end of the day it was 'too community-based' to put on at the Hampstead Theatre. I thought that was quite interesting! These people live in a weird world. They don't have any Asian friends and they don't mix with people from different communities, whereas most of us do, particularly in London. And the added problem is that Asian theatre companies like Tara Arts and Tamasha really only develop new writers on a small scale, although Tamasha's production of Ayub Khan-Din's *East is East* was a huge success; but it was a bit of an exception. Their work is usually based around reinterpreting the classics. And although black theatre companies like Talawa do develop new writers: Biyi Bandele Thomas and Zindika, for example, they don't seem to produce any Asian plays. So there isn't really anywhere for a new writer to go.

In your play *Ananda Sananda*, one of the biggest themes is the need to explore the past and one's roots in order to find an identity and core. Do you feel strongly that Madhu's generation of Indian émigrés and their children need to return to their homeland in some way in order to reclaim their heritage and their whole selves?
When I first started writing I was adamant that I was not going to write about being torn between two cultures. I thought, 'It's so passé and boring.' But inevitably, everything you end up writing is about trying to get that character to search out their roots. It's always about confusion and identity crisis. And I'm quite interested in that middle-class, Indian generation of people who, like my parents, came over in the early sixties. They were educated people and very keen to take on English culture. I was lucky in that my parents were also very proudly Indian. My father used to sing and my mother used to dance and they kept our culture alive. They performed Tagore dance dramas. But a lot of my contemporaries were not even taught Bengali at home. They were brought up in a very English way, a way that would make them comfortable in this society. Their parents were doing it to help them, I suppose. But a lot of them now feel very lost.

The play is also an examination of the clash between Western culture and its soullessness and the more magical and spiritual

Eastern mysticism. Do you think the West has lost its way, with its obsession with time, money and status?

Yes, definitely. The West has lost an awful lot, especially in terms of family values. But beyond that, I'm quite interested in magical realism. A lot of the things I'm writing now have a ghost hanging around them somewhere. It's that whole thing about spirituality and getting in touch with that. My father died six years ago and when he died my writing started. He was a very good writer, but it was always closeted away. I used to say, 'For God's sake, publish your stuff,' but he never did, so it was almost like a determination on my part. And I'm certainly fascinated by things like Hindu mysticism. I don't think it means that you have to believe in God, because I don't, but I like all the myths, the culture. My mum's got a fantastic library of ghost stories in her head, and there's nothing better than sitting by the fire listening to her tell all these. There is a certain lyricism and mysticism about Indian people who live, or have lived, in India. Their language is very philosophical. They don't say, 'Go down the road and buy yourself a loaf of bread.' They say, 'If you go down the road, you'll see that there's a flower shop. Smell the jasmine and then walk across.' It's a very sensual and beautiful-sounding language. It's full of alliteration and it works very well on stage.

Voices on the Wind is based on a true story about your family. Was it difficult to dramatise because of this? And how have your family responded to your dramatisation?

They responded really positively. But then, you see, a lot of them are dead anyway! That was a difficulty with *Voices on the Wind* because it was based so much on what happened. The only difference was that the Irish gaoler didn't really exist. I was constantly having to battle with doing a fictionalisation that was also true to life. But it was enjoyable because I had all the original letters that Dinesh Gupta wrote from prison. He was my grandfather's brother, but he was only nineteen when he was hanged by the British. The first time I went to India, when I was nine years old, I was taken to my grandfather's house and I met his two older brothers. Instead of saying, 'Hello,' they sat me down, got Dinesh Gupta's glasses out and said, 'This is your uncle. He was a freedom fighter for India. These are his glasses and this is a photo they took of him the day before they hanged him.' I remember it so clearly. I remember looking at his glasses and wondering, 'What am I doing looking at a dead man's glasses?' But *Voices on the Wind* was the first thing I ever wrote.

I did find it difficult to characterise him. Normally, you invent a personality for a character, but I was in such awe of this great uncle. I kept thinking, 'My God, at the age of nineteen he did this. Oh my God, how am I going to characterise him?' That's what was so nice about workshopping it at the National Theatre Studio, because I could step back and see the relationship between the Irish gaoler and him, and it wasn't my uncle, but a character.

Why was it important for you to emphasise the significance of violent opposition in the winning of Indian independence?
Because even though there was peaceful, passive resistance with Mahatma Gandhi and Nehru, which was extremely important, there were also a huge number of revolutionaries who went around dropping bombs on the British. The impression you always get about the way that Indian independence was gained is that Mahatma Gandhi went on a few hunger strikes and the British felt so guilty that they thought, 'Oh yes, okay, you can have your country back.' But in the meantime what happened is that hundreds and hundreds of political prisoners were tortured to death. That side of the coin is never, ever shown. But I was certainly not interested in glorifying the violence because, in a way, it was also quite sad. These young men were more or less brainwashed into doing what they did. But I still think it's important to recognise that there was that violence.

The play also examines the consequences of martyrdom for the martyr and his or her family, setting up an important debate about whether we should live life for those immediately around us, or serve the greater good, even if it means tragedy and pain in the short term. What interested you about this debate?
Because it actually happened to my family. The whole family were thrown out of Calcutta. My great-uncle, as a barrister, was not allowed to practise and my grandfather, who was a doctor, was sent off to work on the railway lines. So my father and his entire family grew up on the move and it was as a direct consequence of Dinesh Gupta. The family was basically split up and thrown to the winds. But what was nice was that after independence they all came back to Calcutta and they renamed the road that they had lived in 'Dinesh Gupta Road'. They came home, and however much they'd been affected by Dinesh Gupta's martyrdom, it didn't matter to them. They were always proud of him.

How much pressure do you feel as an Asian writer and as a

**woman writer to focus on certain issues in your work? Or are
you determined to break free of any expectations or labelling?**
I think to a certain extent you label yourself. A lot of the stuff I
did at the beginning was very Asian and very women-orientated.
I think now I'm interested in branching out a bit more, although I
don't want to deviate too much. I've been writing for *Grange Hill*
recently, which is good fun, because it's mainstream, but also, at
the end of the day, there's not a single Asian character in it, and
you think, 'Hang on. How can you have a school in the East End
of London without a single Asian character?' It's nice to be
employed as a writer and not as an Asian writer, but you do think,
'Please, at least give us one Asian.' I don't want to be in a situation
where I'm writing about things that don't really relate to me. But
I'd certainly like to do more integrated stuff. I really liked *The
Buddha of Suburbia*, where there was a cross-section of Asians and
black people and mixed-race people on screen. I remember
watching it, thinking, 'God, that is so rare. You hardly ever see
that on telly,' although it's happening more, I think. But you certainly don't see it on the stage. You see some cross-casting, but the
parts aren't written for us.

**You are probably one of the only Asian women playwrights
working in this country. How can we encourage more to write?**
Well there are a few more around, but they haven't had the breaks
yet. I think they will eventually. Things like workshops help. I had
a mentor, Frances-Anne Solomon who was at the BBC. She more
or less commissioned me and got me where I am. It's the old
network and it's getting in. A lot of people writing these days don't
understand that you have to get in there and sell yourself. Go to
workshops, meet people. I was talking to Judith Johnson and she
was saying that's exactly what she did. I think if there were more
workshops around that welcomed Asian women playwrights, then
that would help. I came from the Asian Writers' Collective and that
was where I got the confidence, the belief that I could write. You
do need to be able to show your work to people that you trust.
The Arts Council are looking at the idea of training some Asian
dramaturgs to do the job of working specifically with new Asian
writers, but they don't understand that there *are* Asian dramaturgs
right under their noses. That's how *Voices on the Wind* started. I
sent it to Sita Brahmachari, Talawa's education officer. She was the
one who picked it up. That's what she did with the women writers
project, she picked up plays and developed them. As far as I can

see she is a dramaturg, but because she's the education officer, she's not recognised. The talent is there, but it needs support.

You are currently Writer-in-Residence at the Soho Theatre Company and are working on a commissioned play, *Flesh and Blood*, for Birmingham Rep. Do you see your future as a theatre writer?
I really do like the theatre. I prefer it above all other mediums. From a writer's perspective, I think writing for the stage is the most pleasurable. It's more skilful; to actually write a play, where you can't blackout, where you have to continue and sustain an audience and a narrative. In the 'old' days people were writer-apprentices in the theatre and then they went off to television. Now, it's the other way round, because it's so difficult to get on stage. I don't know if I see my future in the theatre; it depends if my work continues to get put on. But I'd like to.

Judith Johnson

Judith Johnson's hard-hitting realism has won her much deserved praise. Gutsy, humorous and perceptive characterisation is a feature of all her work, as is her commitment to ordinary, working-class lives, the struggles of youth and the unemployed. She started writing plays in 1987 and has a teaching practice at a Hackney boys' school to thank for making her the playwright that she is today. Not only did it help her to 'round' her male characters, but, in her own words, 'I wrote a lot coming out of that experience. It influenced my whole life. I decided not to be a teacher, but to be a writer instead.' She honoured her debt by writing a number of plays for young people including *The Scrappie* (Red Ladder 1991), *Los Escombros* (Royal National Theatre Education Department, 1992) and *Connected* (Y-Touring Theatre Company, 1994). Her first full-length play, *Working Away*, won the Second Wave Young Women's Writing Festival at the Albany Empire and was produced at the Soho Poly Theatre in 1989.

Judith's other plays include: *Nowheresville* (shortlisted for the Verity Bargate Award in 1991); *Somewhere* (Liverpool Playhouse and the Royal National Theatre, 1993); *Stone Moon* (BT National Connections, 1995); and most recently the widely acclaimed *Uganda* (Royal Court Theatre Upstairs, 1995). Her radio plays include: *Swiftlines and Sweetdreams* (shortlisted for the LBC/Crown FM London Radio Playwrights Competition, 1990); *Octopus Boys* (BBC Radio 5); and *Motorbike Man* (LBC). For television she has written *A Better Life Than Mine* (as part of Carlton's *Going Underground* series) and episodes of *The Bill* and *Grange Hill*. *Somewhere* appears in FRONTLINE INTELLIGENCE, VOL. 1 and *Uganda* in FRONTLINE INTELLIGENCE, VOL. 3, both published by Methuen. She is currently working on a new stage play.

* * *

Personal experience seems to greatly influence your work. How much of it is autobiographical? And do you think your Liverpool

upbringing has helped to give you such a talent for comic dialogue?

I'm not from Liverpool. I'm the other side of the water actually, but quite often that's put in publicity. I'm a fake scouser really. The only play I've written that was directly from personal experience was *Uganda* and that was really hard to write. I mean, I needed to write it, because it was about me dad. I never really intended it to go beyond me writing it as a sort of therapy thing, but it took on a life of its own. I think drawing from personal experience for most writers is your wealth of material really, because we've all got so many stories.

I'm glad you think my dialogue's comic. When I first started writing, I really did try and write funny plays, but then I stopped. It's harder to do it if you're trying to do it. My work is more personal observation; people and the fixes that they get themselves into. My characters are amalgamations of people usually. *Somewhere* was about a gang of teenagers, but I suppose it was to do with when I was a teenager. The main character, Dawn, was just like everyone's tough girl, you know, the real hard-nut girl at school. I wanted her and Lee Kelly, her boyfriend, to be a bit mythological really, you know, icons. The first play I wrote was entirely about a woman who lived across the road from me, but I think it's wrong in a way to do that, because you're pinching someone else's life.

You address a range of important social issues in your work and always through real, domestic, everyday situations, making the personal very political. Why do you choose to do this?

I just do things that way. The degree course I did was theatre and education, drama and the community, so a lot of it's the legacy of that. We looked at a lot of those issues. I think I used to be more politically motivated than I am now, but I've never been party-political, I've always preferred that 'politics is personal' thing. I think about character more than issue and my politics come through the character, although I don't tend to sit and think, 'Oh, my personal politics are this.' The only thing that I really, consciously want to do is look at people's lives and try to understand them, because I think we've got a lot of problems that we've got to understand, each of us. But I don't think it's up to me to offer a solution or to tell other people what they should be looking at.

You seem to be on a mission to put ordinary, working-class lives

back on the stage. Do you think the theatre has become too middle-class in its outlook and values?

It has been for a long time, hasn't it? But recently I think it's got quite a lot better. I suppose since I've been writing it's got better actually. I remember thinking that the National Theatre really should do more plays about ordinary people, that don't necessarily get a big audience, but it's not necessarily true, because, in a way, the audience they are appealing to have got the money to pay for tickets. Theatre is a middle-class pursuit, really. Only certain people go to the theatre, unless it's the pantomime at Christmas, or something that's coming to their school or that one of their kids is in; so even if I'm writing about ordinary, working-class people, it doesn't necessarily lie comfortably with me. People think writers sit down and think, 'Right, I'm going to do this, or I'm going to do that,' but the majority of writers are driven to write about what they're writing about, whether it's from their own personal demons, or personal interest, or things that they don't understand and are trying to understand. There are a few people who sit down and have set agendas and points they want to get across. In the late sixties and seventies there was a lot of that, but not so much now. But I think Sarah Kane, for example, definitely wants to do certain things with her work. There's more of that starting to happen again, but I think we've gone through a period where that wasn't so important. The important work that I do now is theatre in education.

Because you have a real effect on their lives?

I don't know if anything can have a real effect on anybody's life, other than large amounts of money, family background, schooling, but I think it's a really useful educational aid. It's a learning aid and a platform for discussion and I think the important thing about it is that it's a certain type of cultural experience that they don't necessarily get otherwise. Because live performance is not a part of our lives anymore. For thousands of years it was and not only formally in theatres, but informally, in that there were storytellers, which still exists today but it's been watered down, because we don't pay much attention to stories, we watch the box instead.

All your plays feature at least one strong, female character who is living out her feminism naturally, but who comes up against chauvinistic prejudices. Do you deliberately set out to challenge these when you're writing?

Yeah. Probably. It's funny, we were talking about this at the Arvon

Foundation. I was saying you write from your subconscious and that if you think about it too much, then it wrecks it. But Winsome Pinnock was saying that she thinks that that's a conscious decision and that you are actually quite aware of what you're doing. It's like you hold it back for your own benefit to help you write it, in order to make it a storytelling experience for yourself. I've been thinking a lot about that lately, because I'd always thought that things came out naturally, but now I'm trying to think about how conscious it is. The plays do challenge chauvinistic prejudices in a lot of ways, because I'm more brave when I'm writing than I am in real life.

***Somewhere* is, among other things, a powerful play about love and what love is, and Dawn ultimately chooses self-love over the stability, but dependency, she has with Barry and the obsessive, violent love that Lee offers. Is she your role-model for modern woman?**
Not my role-model. She might be somebody else's. I think she used to be mine, but she's that way because of the way that she's been brought up and the things that have happened to her. She's much more independent and strong than I would be. I like lovey-dovey relationships personally. I think I might have spent quite a long time trying to be like her. But I never succeeded! She is a good role-model for some people, but I don't think her ultimate choice is something for everyone. Relationships are funny, aren't they? People are in them for all sorts of reasons, depending on all sorts of things. I try not to judge really. But Dawn does well by the end of the play. She gets a grip.

In *Somewhere* you also look at the consequences of the Thatcher years and long-term unemployment on a group of school-leavers. What inspired that?
Just from my own teenage years and looking at what had happened to people. The age group in the play's a little bit younger than mine. I think I just caught the end of the seventies' free-love, hippy-thing. But people who were three years below me at school went straight into it and immediately went into being punks. They didn't have the benefit of the real welfare state and were cynical from an early age. The eighties, for people who were going from teenagers to adults, were really difficult and dreary and lacking hope. No 'Free love. We can change things.' It was nihilistic really. And while people who had a few bob were living it up and drinking champagne every day, having a good time and making lots of money, a lot of

people were just totally without hope. And, of course, Ecstasy hadn't started, so there wasn't even that to cheer people up. It was very violent. People were into the cult of fighting and it was really just a way of getting aggression out. And, of course, crime thrived, because that's where the jobs were. When I think about that time now, I think of it as being really hopeless and grey and people feeling trapped and not having an outlet. So *Somewhere* was to do with that and what people did to get out of that.

In all your plays, your characters are battling to make something of their lives, but the odds are stacked against them. Only a few manage to transcend their depression to become what they want to. Are you optimistic about the future?
Those early plays were written in that time that we've just talked about. Then when I wrote *Uganda* I'd lost my mother and was trying to deal with a father who was totally grief-stricken. I do see hope for the future because people will try and try. Very few commit suicide, but I had a couple of friends where the odds were stacked quite highly against them and that upset me a lot, for a long time. But people do have that human warmth in them really and they want to share it. There might be hidden layers of mistrust, but the warmth is there; witness the amount of people who keep animals. Everyone wants to love something.

The Toxteth riots in *Working Away* offer a potent symbol of hope and change and the holiday camp becomes a microcosm of society when its own riots break out. Why did you set up this comparison?
Because it happened to me actually. I worked at Butlins while the Toxteth riots were on. Half the staff were scousers and these riots were going on and it was all very exciting and they weren't involved. There were a number of things going on with security staff, so we just had our own mini riot. It was the last night of the season. I wanted to put over the joy of rioting, which is quite dodgy really, because people get quite badly hurt and businesses are wrecked, but I wanted people to understand the relief that comes and the excitement. We had a whale of a time. We'd spent the season being poorly paid and being treated like shit and it felt good going round and wrecking a few places. I mean I didn't do much. I set off a fire-alarm!

So you weren't trying to draw direct parallels with the Toxteth riots?

Well, kind of. I mean, it came out of people being pissed off with police harassment, but once it had started a whale of a time was had by large amounts of people. It's a typically English thing, isn't it? We can't seem to let ourselves go except in extreme acts, like rioting, or getting totally pissed out of our heads. We're not Spanish. We don't fiesta. We're quite restricted really. So I think when the chance comes, we just go mad.

Lack of mutual understanding and breakdown in communication feature prominently in *Uganda*. Did you want to suggest that these things are at the root of larger-scale problems such as racism and war? And did you want to emphasise that answerability lies in us all, that we can't divorce ourselves from what we see on the TV news?

Billy thought that, but he couldn't display the state that he was in. He couldn't put that into practice and that was quite sad. I think I probably did want to suggest that actually. But it was also to do with Billy showing lots of concern and being interested in things that were happening on the TV on the other side of the world, but refusing to engage with the things that were happening in his own front room. It was incredible the number of people who saw it and spoke to me about their fathers. I mean, what's going on with that generation of men? It's really sad.

But also, the way that family misunderstood one another, on a larger scale you end up in a civil war situation, because misunderstanding is at the root of that, at a very basic level.

That's what happens when a certain part of the fabric goes missing. In that family the mother had gone, and everyone had spoken through her, particularly the father. Yugoslavia was fairly stable for years, then there was a change of government and it all fell apart. Things are often held together very fragilely and you just don't realise it. It happened across Eastern Europe, when the Wall came down and communism failed. It was turmoil. And I think if someone is removed from a family, it can be fantastically cathartic, but it can be painful. I got to know my dad very well when my mum died, but if he had died first that would never have happened. I suppose the play is mainly to do with that really.

***Uganda* started off as a workshop production. How useful was this, and do you think workshops are symptomatic of theatre managements 'playing safe'?**

I think they're brilliant, personally. I mean, I know why people think that. But with both *Somewhere* and *Uganda*, it was all done purely in the interest of making the work better. I don't think anyone was doing it to fob me off. I like going for a workshop first because you learn so much about the craft, but you're sheltered from the public. When I write it's real people in real situations. I'm not writing what's going on on stage really, so I need to go through that thing of seeing dramatically, just to see what works and what doesn't work. I found that invaluable.

You thought of *Uganda* as a small play at one point, didn't you? Why?
Well, I just felt awful about it. It was so personal, exposing. And I thought, 'Well, that's all that really happens. There's a fella sitting in his front room and it's not very interesting.' Some people didn't find it very interesting actually, because it isn't a big theatrical experience. Some writers are very skilled at that kind of grand, theatrical presentation, but I can't write like that. I haven't got enough visual sense. And I spend too many hours in front of the TV instead of working!

Sarah Kane

After completing an MA in Playwriting at Birmingham University, which she says, on reflection, nearly destroyed her as a writer, Sarah Kane exploded onto the London theatre scene in the spring of 1995 with her controversial first play *Blasted* (Royal Court Theatre Upstairs), a horrifying examination of the effects of contemporary war on three people in a Leeds hotel room. Accused of putting audiences through 'a catalogue of lurid on-stage depravity', she was vilified by the press and proclaimed 'the most notorious playwright in Britain'. Unphased by the cacophony of media criticism, she directed her second full-length play, *Phaedra's Love*, at the Gate Theatre, Notting Hill, in May 1996. Her plays demonstrate remarkable insight and clarity. They offer us a powerful warning, by showing the tragic but logical conclusion of humanity's escalating, destructive behaviour. Simultaneously they force us to confront our shared responsibility for the brutal reality which already exists. Still only twenty-six, she pioneers a new generation of playwrights and is uninterested in a direct examination of the gender struggle, which she feels is symptomatic of a much wider malaise. Sarah recently completed her new play *Cleansed* and is currently Writer in Residence at Paines Plough. *Blasted* is published in FRONTLINE INTELLIGENCE, VOL. 2 and *Blasted* and *Phaedra's Love* in a single edition; both by Methuen.

* * *

How do you feel about having been labelled 'the most notorious playwright in Britain'?
I don't really think about it. At the time, it made me laugh. When the press erupted over *Blasted* it was ninety-nine per cent enjoyable, one per cent a pain in the arse, but the fact is that none of the people who wrote those things about me know anything about me or my life, so it really doesn't matter.

Were you surprised by the amount of media attention that

Blasted received, because the play was even discussed on *Newsnight*, wasn't it?

Yes. The week the play opened there was an earthquake in Japan in which thousands of people died, and in this country a fifteen-year-old girl had been raped and murdered in a wood, but *Blasted* got more coverage in some newspapers than either of these events. And I'm not only talking about tabloids. Of course it was surprising, no one ever expects such a response (and if they do then they don't get it), but a lot of it passed me by. I was very well protected by the Court and by Mel [Kenyon]. The tabloids never caught up with me.

Do you think that part of the storm that erupted over your work was because critics and audience alike were in a state of disbelief that the issues of violence and war could be tackled by a woman?

I think it's important not to confuse press with audience. There was media outrage, but it was never a public outcry. And as for whether or not the press response was to do with gender, I'm not sure. That explanation clearly can't be applied to Edward Bond or Howard Brenton whose plays have provoked similar hostility. I suppose the fact that it's a play about a middle-aged male journalist who rapes a young woman and is raped and mutilated himself can't have endeared me to a theatre full of middle-aged male critics.

But much more important than the content of the play is the form. All good art is subversive, either in form or content. And the best art is subversive in form *and* content. And often, the element that most outrages those who seek to impose censorship is form. Beckett, Barker, Pinter, Bond – they have all been criticised not so much for the content of their work, but because they use non-naturalistic forms that elude simplistic interpretation. I suspect that if *Blasted* had been a piece of social realism it wouldn't have been so harshly received. The form and content attempt to be one – the form is the meaning. The tension of the first half of the play, this appalling social, psychological and sexual tension, is almost a premonition of the disaster to come. And when it does come, the structure fractures to allow its entry. The play collapses into one of Cate's fits. The form is a direct parallel to the truth of the war it portrays – a traditional form is suddenly and violently disrupted by the entrance of an unexpected element that drags the characters and the play into a chaotic pit without logical explanation. In terms of Aristotle's Unities, the time and action are disrupted while unity of place is retained. Which caused a great deal of offence because it implied a direct link between domestic violence in Britain and civil war in the former Yugoslavia. *Blasted* raised the question 'What does a common rape in Leeds have to do with mass rape as a war weapon in Bosnia?' And the answer appeared to be 'Quite a lot'. The unity of place suggests a paper-thin wall between the safety and civilisation of peacetime Britain and the chaotic violence of civil war. A wall that can be torn down at any time, without warning.

The press outcry at the images presented wasn't outrage at the idea of such a thing actually happening, but about being asked to consider the idea when viewing that imagery. The shock wasn't about the content, not even about the shock of the new, but about the familiar being arranged in such a way that it could be seen afresh. The press was screaming about cannibalism live on stage, but, of course, audiences weren't looking at actual atrocities, but at an imaginative response to them in an odd theatrical form, apparently broken-backed and schizophrenic, which presented material without comment and asked the audience to craft their own response. The representation of violence caused more anger than actual violence. While the corpse of Yugoslavia was rotting on our doorstep, the press chose to get angry, not about the corpse, but about the cultural event that drew attention to it. That doesn't surprise me. Of course the press wish to deny that what happened in Central Europe has anything to do with us, of course they don't want us to be aware of the extent of the social sickness we're suffering from – the moment they acknowledge it, the ground opens up to swallow them. They celebrate the end of the Cold War then rapidly return to sex scandals (which sell more papers) and all that has been done to secure our future as a species is the reduction of the overkill factor.

When you set out to write a play, how do you want it to affect an audience?
You can't second-guess audiences and you can't control how they will respond to any given theatrical experience. I wouldn't want to try to create a reaction, but you have to know what you want to do to them. What I think about when I'm writing is how I want it to affect me and the best way to achieve that.

Why did you choose to retell the story of *Phaedra*?
The Gate asked me to write a play based on a European classic. I read Seneca's *Phaedra* and was struck by two things. Firstly, that it's a play about a sexually corrupt Royal Family – which makes it

highly contemporary. And secondly, that Hippolytus, as he is in the original story, is deeply unattractive. Though he's physically beautiful, he's chaste, a puritan, a hater of mankind. For me, puritanism isn't about lifestyle, but an attitude. Instead of pursuing what is traditionally seen as pure, my Hippolytus pursues honesty, both physically and morally – even when that means he has to destroy himself and everyone else. The purity of his self-hatred makes him much more attractive as a character than the virginal original. There was also something about the inadequacy of language to express emotion that interested me. In *Phaedra's Love*, what Hippolytus does to Phaedra is not rape – but the English language doesn't contain the words to describe the emotional decimation he inflicts. 'Rape' is the best word Phaedra can find for it, the most violent and potent, so that's the word she uses.

You are continually accused of using gratuitous violence, and the whole purpose of your plays, to confront the reality of violence and abuse, seems to pass unnoticed, especially where the critics are concerned. Do you think *Blasted* and *Phaedra's Love* have been misunderstood?
There's been a failure by the critical establishment to develop an adequate language with which to discuss drama. A list of contents is not a review, but that is, almost without fail, what new plays receive – a brief synopsis with a note at the end saying whether or not this story was pleasing to the reviewer. So of course they fail to understand any play which refuses to sloganise. On a certain level, it doesn't matter – whether the critics say you're a genius or they say you're a depraved monster; they don't make the job of writing any harder or any easier. Nothing they say is of any relevance. It's always as hard as it is, and there's very little that anyone can say to change that. However, critics do have the power to kill a show dead with their cynicism, and I regret that they don't take their jobs as seriously as the writers they so frequently and casually try to destroy.

The critic John Peter raised an important question with regard to your work. He asked, 'How much despair can you convey and how much horror can you show before an audience is overdosed?' Is this something you are aware of when you are writing?
Most people experience a lot more despair and brutality than John Peter would like to believe. There's only the same danger of overdose in the theatre as there is in life. The choice is either to represent

it, or not to represent it. I've chosen to represent it because sometimes we have to descend into hell imaginatively in order to avoid going there in reality. If we can experience something through art, then we might be able to change our future, because experience engraves lessons on our hearts through suffering, whereas speculation leaves us untouched. And anyone – politician, journalist, artist – who attempts to give people that imaginative experience, faces defensive screams that it's too much from all sectors of the artistic and political spectrum. It's crucial to chronicle and commit to memory events never experienced – in order to avoid them happening. I'd rather risk overdose in the theatre than in life. And I'd rather risk defensive screams than passively become part of a civilisation that has committed suicide.

How much influence do you think your plays can have, in terms of changing society's perceptions and actions?
I've seen one piece of theatre that changed my life – Jeremy Weller's *Mad*. It changed my life because it changed me – the way I think, the way I behave, or try to behave. If theatre can change lives, then by implication it can change society, since we're all part of it. I also think it's important to remember that theatre is not an external force acting on society, it's part of it, a reflection of the way people within that society view the world. Slasher movies don't create a violent society (though they may well perpetuate it), they're a product of that society. Films, books, theatre, they all represent something which already exists, even if only in someone's head, and through that representation they can change or reinforce what they describe.

Is that why you write?
Yes.

In both your plays and in the world at large, it is essentially men who perpetuate violence. Is this something which you purposely set out to explore?
No. My main source of thinking about how violence happens is myself, and in some ways all of my characters are me. I write about human beings, and since I am one, the ways in which all human beings operate is feasibly within my understanding. I don't think of the world as being divided up into men and women, victims and perpetrators. I don't think those are constructive divisions to make, and they make for very poor writing.

How was the experience of directing *Phaedra's Love* yourself?
Terrifying. But I loved it. Sometimes during *Blasted* I wasn't seeing exactly the image I'd written and I couldn't understand why. I thought I should find out just how hard it is to realise my own images, because it's one of those things I can never make any concessions about. So I was terrified of letting the writer down. I knew she'd give me a really hard time if I did.

The staging was interesting, with the audience sitting all over the theatre and the actors emerging from the middle of them. Why did you choose to stage it like that?
It wasn't as conscious as this, but I think it meant that for any given audience member, the play could be at one moment intimate and personal, at the next epic and public. They may see one scene from one end of the theatre and find themselves sitting in the middle of a conversation for the next. And since it is a play that becomes more and more public, that's an entirely appropriate experience to have.

In *Phaedra's Love*, your female characters are the most under-developed and receive the least emphasis. Was this because your main concern was to attack the whole patriarchal system, the hypocrisy and fundamental corruption of state, church and monarchy?
I'd dispute the assertion that the women are underdeveloped. And I'm sure the actresses who played them would too. Phaedra is the first person to become active in the play – her accusation and suicide liberate Hippolytus and set off the most extraordinary chain of events leading to the collapse of the monarchy. But I'm not writing about sexual politics. The problems I'm addressing are the ones we have as human beings. An over-emphasis on sexual politics (or racial or class politics) is a diversion from our main problem. Class, race and gender divisions are symptomatic of societies based on violence or the threat of violence, not the cause.

What do you feel your greatest responsibility is as a writer, and as a woman writer?
My only responsibility as a writer is to the truth, however unpleasant that truth may be. I have no responsibility as a woman writer because I don't believe there's such a thing. When people talk about me as a writer, that's what I am, and that's how I want my work to be judged – on its quality, not on the basis of my age, gender, class, sexuality or race. I don't want to be a representative

of any biological or social group of which I happen to be a member.
I am what I am. Not what other people want me to be.

Timberlake Wertenbaker

Razor-sharp observation and a powerful, lyrical language have become the hallmarks of Timberlake Wertenbaker's prolific canon of work, which has attracted numerous awards, including the Laurence Olivier Play of the Year Award and the New York Drama Critics' Circle Award for Best New Foreign Play for *Our Country's Good*. Celebrated widely for the extraordinary vitality of her writing, her expansive vision and the depth with which she treats her themes, she is one of our greatest contemporary playwrights. Her work explores a huge variety of subjects and has asked some of the most important questions of our time, encompassing the value and meaning of art, the quest for power and the seductive appeal of corruption, the effects of enforced silencing, the definition of crime and civilisation and the need for reappraisal in the light of the approaching millennium.

Timberlake's plays include: *The Third* (King's Head, 1980); *Case to Answer* (Soho Poly, 1980); *New Anatomies* (ICA, 1981); *Abel's Sister* (Royal Court Theatre Upstairs, 1983); *The Grace of Mary Traverse* (Royal Court Theatre Downstairs, 1985, which won the *Plays and Players* Most Promising Playwright Award); *Our Country's Good* (which opened at the Royal Court Theatre Downstairs in 1988, and transferred to the West End and Broadway); *The Love of the Nightingale* (Royal Shakespeare Company's Other Place, 1988, which won the 1989 Eileen Anderson Central Television Drama Award); *Three Birds Alighting on a Field* (Royal Court Theatre Downstairs, 1991, which won the Susan Smith Blackburn Prize, Critics' Circle Award and Writers' Guild Award in 1992) and *The Break of Day* (national tour and Royal Court Theatre Downstairs, 1995). An Anglo-American who grew up in the French Basque country, she is a fluent French speaker and has translated a number of plays, including: Marivaux's *False Admissions* and *Successful Strategies* for Shared Experience; Marivaux's *La Dispute*; Ariane Mnouchkine's *Mephisto* (adapted for the RSC); Sophocles' *The Theban Plays* (adapted for the RSC); Euripides' *Hecuba* (for ACT, San Francisco) and Jean Anouilh's *Leocadia* and Maurice Maeterlinck's *Pelleas and Melisande* (both for BBC Radio). Her television and film work includes a screenplay of *The Children*, based on Edith Wharton's novel, and a BBC 2 film entitled *Do Not Disturb. Our Country's Good* is published by Methuen; her translations of Marivaux's plays, *False Admissions, Successful Strategies* and *La Dispute* appear in one volume, published by Absolute Classics); and *The Theban Plays* and *The Break of Day* are both published by Faber & Faber, who have also published a collection of her work, TIMBERLAKE WERTENBAKE: PLAYS.

*   *   *

You are one of the few women playwrights whose work has been regularly produced on main stages. How do you think you have managed to escape being relegated to less prominent spaces, like so many other women playwrights?
I think it's mostly luck and having tall, extremely good actresses in my plays. *The Grace of Mary Traverse* was commissioned by the Theatre Upstairs, and we had a reading there. Janet McTeer is very tall and everyone said, 'No. No. She's too tall for Upstairs. She'll have to go Downstairs.' So that was my first play. Downstairs. That's it. Tall parts.

How important has the Royal Court been to you as a writer, both in terms of nurturing your talent at the beginning and giving you the space to explore?
It's been very important. Again, it was a matter of luck. At the time it was putting on plays that I found very exciting. It was where I wanted to be. It was the first theatre to realise that there were women out there who could write and that there was an audience for those women. For women playwrights it was a terrific time because you could see the work of other women playwrights, which was very interesting. It was a time when women were prominent at the Royal Court. Well, that has obviously changed. There was a certain reaction in the press and suddenly they were hungry for a different kind of play: male violence, homoerotica. There hadn't been much of that before and that's what was wanted. These are slightly more reactionary times and it's not the most welcoming moment for women; there's no question about that. Maybe audiences wanted something else, although I think there is still a hunger for plays by women and about women. It remains to be seen whether the situation changes. I'm sure it will.

Women writers are sorely under-represented though, aren't they, as far as the whole spectrum of British theatre goes?
Yes, and I think that's to do with the fact that, on the whole, the

theatre is still run, and the scene is still commented on, by men. There aren't many women. It's not an equal representation in terms of producers, money, newspapers and so forth. But you can't say that if there were fifty per cent women then theatre would be radically different, because a lot of women directors, for example, choose to put on male playwrights. If you look at that you'd be quite surprised. There are a lot of women who don't particularly want to see what women are writing. Whether that's informed by the culture or whether that's just the way they are, who knows. So you can't guarantee that putting women in fifty per cent of the positions of power is going to change that, but obviously it would help. It wouldn't be a bad idea to try it out.

You have said that you 'live in the imagination, which is not always the most fashionable area for a female dramatist'. What did you mean by this?
I meant that the plays that women are allowed to write – and this is less true now, it was truer when I was first writing – were plays about how rough it is to be a woman; quite realistic, naturalistic plays, often set in a kitchen or a domestic environment. Those plays were safe and were allowed because that wasn't male territory. It was female territory and it wasn't really going to bother anybody. People liked those plays because they showed that women had problems, with love basically. If you tried to branch out and just write plays, it was not that acceptable. I think that has changed, but it hasn't changed as much as I would have liked it to change. I mean, more women playwrights are branching out now and taking on big subjects, but they're not always well received. It's still not considered acceptable territory. Actually that's not *quite* true because the plays I've done have been on big subjects and have been well received, but it doesn't seem to happen enough. It's not encouraged enough. Maybe purely because male playwrights want to keep that territory to themselves.

The playwright Ellen Dryden came up with an interesting observation. She said that 'if a man writes a play about a relationship it is seen as having global significance, but if a woman writes a play about a relationship, it's a play about a relationship.' Do you think that's true?
Yes. I think that's right. But what you have to ask yourself is whether women themselves shy away from giving what they're writing a global significance, making that step, or whether that is shied away from in the production. It's very hard to untangle all

that. I think you have to be careful not to say, 'Women are not allowed to write X because of men,' because I think it's much more complicated than that. The censorship is much more internalised, seriously internalised and then reinforced by what's going on outside. It's unhelpful to feel that it's just because there are a lot of male critics or because the theatre establishment is essentially male, because I think women do internalise this very much and that's the real problem.

But it's still a remarkable thing for a female character to represent universality, in the same way as a male Hamlet does. Is that something that occurred to you with *The Grace of Mary Traverse*?
That's exactly what I wanted to do. I wanted a woman on a quest, a woman who was active. There was an interesting reaction because in the second act when Mary gets up on a soapbox and says all these things about freedom for this and that, I remember one critic saying, 'The play was fine until Wertenbaker starting spouting all this feminist business.' Now, the quotes Mary was using were directly from Tom Paine, but the fact that a *woman* was saying that, and I think unconsciously the fact that I was a woman playwright, turned it all into something feminist. It was feminist, but it was the eighteenth century and it was Tom Paine. I remember spotting that and thinking if it had been a man saying those things, or a male playwright, that criticism would not have been made.

In *New Anatomies*, Lydia says at one point: 'Do you know that in order to write seriously I must dress as a man ... When I am dressed as a woman ... I find I am most concerned with the silky sound of my skirt rustling on the floor ... But when I am dressed as a man I simply begin to think, I get ideas.' Were you interested in exploring the physical and psychological imprisonment of female dress?
The pressure from the magazines to go back to tight skirts and high heels is something that really disturbs me: the fact that you can't walk, and if you can't walk you don't think very well. And the vanity with which we are brought up. The amount of effort that one makes just getting dressed and worrying about appearances is very time-consuming. There's a lot in just being a woman that is extremely distracting and does actually keep you from thinking and writing. There's no question about it. So I was exploring that. Women have to watch their mental make-up, that's what concerns me. And seeing yourself as an object (which I think women do

very much) does of necessity make you think differently. It probably makes you less observant because you're turned in on yourself. I blame society and, of course, I blame magazines, although I'm a great reader of magazines, so I'm very familiar with the problem! I don't want a Maoist state, but I think it's dangerous when women see themselves completely as objects; and we have a great display of that with the Duchess of York and the Princess of Wales, who can only see themselves as they are seen by others. It's quite a phenomenon.

It's up to women to have the strength to defend themselves and censor this. It's down to education and presenting attractive alternatives. That's part of our responsibility as writers, I think, to present alternatives that are attractive and interesting. Isabelle Eberhardt was one of the first women who de-objectified herself, became what she was and went on a quest. I've always liked women on quests. There are too few women on quests in this world. Most heroic male characters, whether it's Peer Gynt or Hamlet, are on a quest for knowledge or self-knowledge and women haven't done enough of that. They stay in place and they are the quested. But she was certainly on a quest and she certainly found something.

And playwriting is a sort of quest in itself. That's the fun bit about being a playwright. Most of it is awful, but that's the good bit. You know, you move through your own subject. You explore it. I don't think women's imagination has been explored enough; what it does when it roams freely. It's not let loose very often and certainly not enough in the theatre.

In *The Grace of Mary Traverse*, you look at the consequences of Mary's choices when she enters into a Faustian pact for knowledge and power. Did you want to show that the possibilities of such a journey and the potential abuse of power are exactly the same for a woman as for a man?
Yes. I was getting annoyed with a lot of the idealism that when women have power the whole world will change. If only. It might change if they have a great deal of self-knowledge at the same time. But the idea that you just get power and then it's all going to be different is naive in the extreme and rather dangerous. It used to irritate me intensely. Power is power. And I think that the end of the twentieth century is going to show that it has to be thought through again: the whole thing that you either give power to the people, or power to women, or to minorities, and then it's all right. It's not that simple. What it is, I don't think we know. But the whole despair at the end of this century is discovering that there

are very few solutions to society and to the abuse of power. It's the madness of human beings. Things have been learnt, but there has, in fact, been an incredible failure all round. And in that sense it's a very interesting time to be watching things, very scary, but very interesting. That's something that feminists have to take on board, that women are not necessarily better by nature.

It's easier to blame someone else.
It is. And I think women have to look very carefully at that. As they gain power, and I hope they have the courage to continue to gain power, they have to know what the failings are. And that's what I wanted to show with Mary, that it would be very easy at that point to get discouraged, which is what happens to her. And women have retreated from the world in the last few years.

Our Country's Good **is a wonderful defence of the theatre and its value to individuals and society, as well as a classic example of how in oppressive times the arts are censored, if not obliterated. You have a strong belief in the redemptive power of art. Can you tell us more about this?**
I think art is redemptive and the theatre is particularly important because it's a public space. That's the crucial element. It's discursive and it's public. And there are very few of those spaces left. I think the English are embarrassed by art. In a society that's not very much in touch with itself, art will be uncomfortable and I think that's the situation in England at the moment. It's an extremely uncomfortable country in all kinds of ways and art is not going to be very appealing in that kind of discomfort. In terrible times you want to learn, which is why art does flourish in appalling circumstances, but in uncomfortable times, in times when people are quite ashamed of themselves, it's not a good time. That doesn't mean that art shouldn't continue and that one shouldn't fight for it. I don't think it's a problem. This desperate plea of, 'Oh everybody really *does* want to go to the theatre.' They don't. But that doesn't matter. Some people will go and they will get something out of it. This need to appeal to the mass is misplaced. People will find the theatre when they need to. It doesn't have to be rammed down throats. People will find it, as long as it's not destroyed. You know, I wish 25,000 people a night attended plays, but they don't. And they won't. But it doesn't mean, therefore, that you should stop writing, or stop putting plays on.

You have said that 'Theatre should not be used to flatter, but

to reveal, which is to disturb.' Is enough of this type of theatre
being produced?
I think it is at the moment. It comes and goes. But what was
disturbing three months ago becomes extremely safe, very quickly.
So, although you think you're being disturbed, in fact, you know
the territory. I think that's happening a little bit right now. There
have been a lot of urban riot plays and they have been disturbing,
but they've become increasingly less disturbing because we're familiar with them. And now we're in danger of having endless urban
riot plays. But every year you get one or two plays that disturb
and you get a lot of safe plays. You don't always know which is
which. Sometimes people are so disturbed by a play that they don't
know they're disturbed; they just don't like the play. There's also
that. Everybody always says, 'Oh the theatre's good this year. The
theatre was bad that year,' but I think, on the whole, the theatre is
about the same every year. And most of it is not very good, though
some of it is wonderful. Most of it is very safe, but I think that's
because it's a very hard form to make work. There's a craft element
in it and because of that, it's very difficult to write a play that's
interesting and different and that's catching something, but at the
same time does work as a play. That's the problem with the theatre.
That's what's exciting about it, but what's also very difficult about
it. You cannot just go haywire, because it won't actually work.

'If you break conventions, it is inevitable that you make
enemies,' says Philip in *Our Country's Good*. 'This play irritates
them.' Does this offer one explanation as to why arts subsidy
has been so seriously eroded?
I think to some extent. Certainly when Mrs Thatcher came into
power it all happened very quickly. It's amazing how powerful the
theatre is in its own small way. You know, the minute something
is threatening it creates a big *brouhaha*, or something's closed down.
I think it's seen as an area where people have too many ideas.

In *Our Country's Good* you also examine crime and punishment,
what constitutes deviance and how the Western notion of 'civilisation' is often the very reverse of what it claims to be, with the
so-called 'civilised' more criminal than the 'criminals'. Were you
putting the contemporary justice system under the microscope?
A little bit. There was a lot of talk when I was writing it about
'born' criminals, just as there had been in the eighteenth century.
It was the beginning of the Michael Howard era, although he wasn't
Home Secretary then. There was quite a lot of talk about that and

I'm not sure if that wasn't also the beginning of the idea that you were genetically criminal. I just found that so distasteful and so familiar. I mean, we've been there before. So I wanted to question that a little bit. It was also the beginning of the devaluation of education. Education has never been valued very highly in this country, but, you know, the idea that you couldn't educate certain people, that it was hopeless. I was very aware of that and keen to attack. It's certainly got much worse since.

In *The Love of the Nightingale*, Philomele and Procne avenge themselves of the atrocities and injustices they have suffered by killing Itys, not Tereus, and they tell Tereus, 'That is the future.' Does the future promise nothing but violence if justice remains absent and all members of society are not given their voice?
I did feel very strongly that if you can't speak, if you don't have the language, the only way you can express yourself is violently, and I think we have evidence of it all around. If you can speak, you can at least make your claims, hope to be listened to, make more claims, listen to the other side. Without that, yes. I think there will be nothing but violence. And the sections of society now, the people who have no voice, are violent, inevitably. If you refuse to listen to a section of society, you are silencing them.

You frequently use the past to explore the present, but more recently you have set your plays very much in the here and now. Has it become more urgent for you to address issues directly, without the filter of the past?
It comes and goes. Sometimes I like looking at the past, sometimes I like looking at the present. I mean, if a play is about the present, if it's specifically about the present, like the art world in *Three Birds Alighting on a Field*, or the subject matter of *The Break of Day*, then you set it in the present. If it's a theme – silence or injustice or whatever – you can set it in the past. If you write things in the past you free them of people's prejudices. You can be more poetic. You tend to be less poetic when it's a contemporary play. You can be more imaginative in the past. It's more fun in some ways, but the present needs to be addressed.

***The Break of Day* forces some disturbing comparisons between infertility and moral barrenness. This whole metaphor and the way in which you develop it is very powerful. What inspired it?**
There were a lot of strands to the play and I wanted to write an absolutely contemporary play about everybody's situation; the end

of the century, in a way. I was trying to get at something that was very immediate. I didn't have a conclusion or a simple line for others to see, I was just exploring as I was writing: you know, the fatigue at the end of the century, the breakdown of a lot of ideals, particularly for women, and this notion of the future and what the future is, what sort of future we are providing for others.

A *Daily Mail* critic scathingly commented in his review of *The Break of Day* that 'Big issues do not important dramas make'. Most critics were unable to take your questioning on board and dismissed the play. Do you think they have lost sight of what theatre is, and can be?
They didn't make the effort to understand it, which shocked me actually, because I think they should have made that effort. I mean, some did, but most didn't. You know, it's very hard to know why theatre critics decide they won't tackle something. And I'm not going to sit here and say, 'They're all stupid. They don't understand,' or, 'They hate women,' because I don't think that's correct. They just couldn't see it with this play. Maybe it was too complicated. Maybe it was an unpopular subject, I don't know. If you go to the theatre a lot, you don't always want a difficult evening. There is that. And critics say it themselves, they get tired. Critics do stay a long time in their jobs now and some remain fantastically enthusiastic forever, but some do not. I mean, we have a generation of critics who have been in their posts for a long time. They may be a bit tired. But if you changed all the critics would things be any better? It's always been a problem, the critics and the playwrights. Sometimes it goes well. I've had my share of good reviews and I've had my share of appalling reviews. When they give good reviews they're very intelligent and when they give bad reviews they're very stupid! They like to give bad reviews. They like to put you down a bit. But I have to say I was extremely upset and quite shocked by their unwillingness to look at that play, particularly because it was a contemporary play and I felt I was dealing with something important. That's the down side of the theatre. You're out there and you're very exposed.

You usually start your plays with a question and your characters constantly question themselves, but you have said that playwrights should not be expected to 'have the answers. If you really have the answers, you shouldn't be a writer but a politician.' How do you define the role of the playwright?
I think the playwright writes plays. In other words, you try to

grapple with, you try to make a narrative of, however disjointed, what you're seeing and present it in more of an argument form than an imaginative narrative, which is the novel. I think, because the theatre is a public arena, playwrights should use that. You know, when I hear people saying, 'Oh I hate ideas in plays,' I think, 'Well, just don't go to the theatre.' It drives me crazy. It's wonderful to have visual stuff, but if you don't have ideas or argument or conflict or debate, forget it. That's what the theatre is best at. I suppose a writer tries to filter something in a deeper way than a journalist and tries to pull the strands together. It's a very hard job at the minute because it's such a confused moment. That's why we particularly need playwrights now and especially women playwrights, because they have many fewer prejudices, fewer fore-gone conclusions than male playwrights. It's important for women to put themselves out there.

Marina Carr

One of the most original talents to have emerged from the Irish stage in recent years, Marina Carr is a writer passionately committed to the magic of theatre. Her styles of dramatisation and her characters are as diverse as her boundless and haunting imagination, which has created both the enigmatic and tragic Portia Coughlan and the one-hundred-year-old, opium-smoking Grandma Fraochlan of *The Mai*. Born in 1964 and brought up in Tullamore, County Offaly, Marina graduated from University College, Dublin, with a degree in English and Philosophy, taught in New York for a year and started a Masters Degree on Samuel Beckett before putting that aside when her playwriting career took off. Her first play, *Ullaloo*, was presented as a rehearsed reading at the Dublin Theatre Festival in 1989 and received a full production at the Abbey Theatre's Peacock in 1991. Her second play, *Low in the Dark*, a Beckettian-influenced tragi-comedy which explored the issue of gender-stereotyping, was performed at the Project Arts Centre, Dublin, in 1989 and in 1994 her celebrated play *The Mai* received much critical acclaim when it was staged at the Peacock Theatre. It went on to win the Dublin Theatre Festival's Best New Irish Play Award and was revived on the Abbey Theatre's main stage in 1995, following a successful run at the Tron Theatre, Glasgow. In 1996 her powerful, lyrical voice finally gained widespread recognition in London when *Portia Coughlan* (which won the Susan Smith Blackburn Prize for 1997) transferred from the Abbey Theatre to the Royal Court's main stage, where it met with rave reviews. *The Independent* referred to 'the maturing of a hugely valuable dramatic voice'. Following this success, *The Mai* was produced at the Tricycle Theatre in April 1997.

Marina is currently Ansbacher Writer-in-Association at the Abbey Theatre and has recently been made a member of Aosdana, an Irish government body which gives a lifetime income to artists. She is working on three new plays, *On Raftary's Hill*, *Ariel* and *By the Bog of Colts*.

Low in the Dark appears in an anthology entitled THE CRACK IN THE EMERALD (Nick Hern Books); *Portia Coughlan* in Faber & Faber's THE DAZZLING DARK anthology and in a single text edition, published by Faber & Faber, who are also planning an anthology of her work.

* * *

When you first start writing a play, where do you begin? What is the initial inspiration that starts the creative process? And how do you build on this?
It's different all the time. The first three or four plays I was heavily influenced by Beckett. The whole absurdist idea appealed to me very much and it still does. I'd like to go back to that at some stage. *The Mai* was part autobiography, part creation. You use a hook to start off and then you write and write and write. It's such a sly craft. In a sense, all you need is one image, or a couple of dislocated images, and you try and bind them together. With *Portia Coughlan* it was a childhood friend whom I'd heard a story about. I hadn't seen her in about fifteen years, but I heard a story about her from my brother who still visits the area I was brought up in, and that started all that. Also *The Merchant of Venice*, which was the first Shakespeare play I ever studied at school. It's so difficult to know what begins a play – you know, the story about the friend, a Shakespeare passage, the Midland landscape. You start imagining a situation and you take it up a pitch or down a few notches.

I spend a lot of time thinking. With *Portia Coughlan*, which was commissioned by the National Maternity Hospital, they gave me a room in the hospital and my routine would be to get up at ten or eleven o'clock, go into town, have coffee for about two or three hours and then go in and write the scene. But I'd have been 'writing' the scene throughout that time. I've found this coffee shop where they're great to me. They just let me sit and space away. Then the actual writing of the scene happens in about an hour, an hour and a half. But the work is almost all done with the mulling. It's not like a logical thing though, 'So-and-so says this and so-and-so says that.' It's like free-wheeling; letting things pass through, letting things pass in or out.

Are the characters quite shaped before you sit down to write?
They should be. There have been times when they aren't and it shows; when you haven't actually got a hold on them. You know Ibsen's passage on writing a play? With the first draft he knew his characters as you might after a train journey. With the second he saw everything more clearly, as though he'd spent a week with them at a spa, and by the last draft he knew them as his intimate

friends, from a long association. It's that kind of thing. I think if you can get your first draft down without a crucial fault line, without an irreparable fault line, you're all right. The rest will come. If there's a crucial fault line in the first draft then you might as well throw it in the bin. And you only know that by writing it. You can't plan out the beginning, middle and end. Well, I can't because all the discovery is gone then.

It's a real journey in every sense.
Yeah, it is. Or it should be. I suppose to trust that is the most difficult. Sometimes you don't and you try to manipulate and squeeze and it always shows. The most difficult thing to accomplish is to let the characters write themselves, rather than you imposing on them.

Your characters express an extraordinary range of emotion, some of it very dark. Where does this depth come from?
In one sense, you could say it's finally all about yourself. You lead so many lives. So many. I can only count back maybe four or five thoughts that have gone through me at any given time. When you think of just an hour of space and what you come up with, all the range of emotions from dark to light, from the hilarious to the really tragic. There are a thousand lives in each of us. There's this huge history that you're only peripherally aware of. Dreams help me a lot. It's like a whole life going on while you're asleep. If you could be vigilant enough to record all of them, you'd have a story with each one. Writing from the unconscious seems the best place, of course tempered with the conscious, but I think it's the truest. Writing isn't about being an intellectual or about being an academic. I think very often it's confused with academia, but it's a very different source. Of course, it helps to read a bit and know where you're coming from, but I think it's more about things you can't understand than things you can.

Your writing has a powerful, lyrical quality about it and is essentially non-naturalistic. How much of this do you put down to your Irish heritage?
Well, lyric sensibility is not just an Irish thing. It's a certain type of writing. You have playwrights who are poets of the theatre and playwrights who aren't and the kind of writing I would aspire to would be of a lyric sensibility: Tennessee Williams, Chekhov, Shakespeare. A lot of contemporary playwrights would not be poets of the theatre. It's a different kind of prose theatre writing,

which is very valid in itself, but it's not the kind of writing that appeals to me. Of course, it's a very Irish thing as well. How we tell a story is so important. It's not facts you're looking for, it's the details, the embellishments. I think most Irish people know how to tell a story instinctively and tell it well. We're very aware of the metaphor here and use it at any given opportunity!

Benedict Nightingale commented in his *Times* review of *Portia Coughlan* that '*Portia Coughlan* will probably be called melodramatic, but only because we live in an imaginatively timid age and Carr dares a lot'. What are your feelings about this?

I would agree with him. It is. Everything has become factual. What has happened to the whole idea of magic in theatre? I mean, very often what you see now will be two episodes of a sitcom or soap opera. It's like the more television-influenced something is, the better it is. Everything is judged by the television god and we've forgotten standards. The yardstick has been lost. I find that really abhorrent, but I think, at the same time, there are enough people out there who realise. You should know your classics. You should know what the standards are and then see how you can measure up to them because there are so many great plays which are entirely theatrical.

In *The Mai* you explore the repetitive cycle of family destruction, as Grandma Fraochlan says, 'We repeat and we repeat. The orchestration may be different, but the tune is always the same.' What is it about this that fascinates you?

Well, I suppose the whole idea of destiny and personal freedom. I'm a bit confused about that. I don't know how much free choice there actually is and how much you're conditioned by those who have gone before you. I'm constantly finding things out about myself that are so like my mother and my father and my grandparents, and I think that's something that needs to be examined; just for living, let alone writing. Just what you are repeating?

Why did you choose Millie as the narrator of the story, a story which, while it has a profound effect upon her, she doesn't fully partake in?

Why did I choose Millie? Because the stakes are high for her. She's the first one of them that's beginning to put the pieces together. Not in any kind of complete way, but she's beginning to ask questions that the other women in the family accepted or took for granted. I'm not saying she's right, but she's beginning to ask. I also wanted to write a play with a narrator in it. I'd been reading *The Glass Menagerie*, a play I love, and a little bit of Chekhov as well. Unfortunately I wasn't enough influenced by them! I suppose I was trying to tell a story from all the different perspectives. People have asked me of *The Mai*: 'Who is the lead character, is it Grandma Fraochlan, is it the Mai or is it Millie?' I kind of like that actually. The ambiguity. Some people would see that as a fault and I take their point. You know, if you call a play *The Mai*, then shouldn't the title of the play be your main character? But I think she is the centre of the play. They all come to her, and they all go from her. It is essentially her story. I didn't want Millie to take over. That's why I didn't begin the play with a narrator. I wanted the Mai to begin the play and the Mai to end it. But I wanted Millie to, I suppose, have her say within that. Finally, she's just a storyteller. She's telling the story, at a slant. In the first couple of drafts I wrote, Millie was quite factual, filling in scene to scene, but then I realised that you don't need that. What you need are stories coming in at a slant that will throw a light. I was quite happy with the outcome.

Grandma F. says: 'I would gladly a hurlt all seven a ye down tha slopes a hell for wan nigh' more wud tha nine-fingered fisherman an' may I roh eternally for such unmotherly feelin'.' In most of your work you portray women who are lovers first and mothers second. Is that incidental, or are you saying that not all women are natural mothers and that motherhood is not necessarily all that it's cracked up to be?
I don't think the world should assume that we are all natural mothers. And it does. I don't think it's such a big thing anymore, but the idea that you sacrifice everything for your children – it's a load of rubbish. It leads to very destructive living and thinking, and it has a much worse effect on children than if you go out and live your own life. You're meant to adore your children at all times, and you're not meant to have a bad thought about them. That's fascism, you know, and it's elevating the child at the expense of the mother. It's like your life is not valid except in fulfilling this child's needs. What about all your needs, your desires, your wants, your problems? They're going to come out anyway, so it's better they're acknowledged straight off. Having said that, I really do believe that children have to be protected. They have to be loved. Somewhere between the two, I think, something needs to be sorted out. The relationship between parent and child is so difficult and so complex. There's every emotion there. We mostly only acknowledge the good

ones. If we were allowed to talk about the other ones, maybe it would alleviate them in some way.

The Mai says that Grandma F. brought them up with too much hope, 'her stories made us long for something extraordinary to happen in our lives.' This is true of all your characters who end up disillusioned and heartbroken.
I suppose, yeah. I don't think there's anyone alive who doesn't want something extraordinary to happen. Isn't that what we're all waiting for? It's about trying to live in the present. Everything is the past or future. I haven't mastered that one. People who have, I think, are extraordinary people. Happy people. It's an inbuilt mechanism in every individual to want the extraordinary, the un-reachable, the impossible. The thing is, heartbreak shouldn't kill you. But then we're talking about theatre. We're talking about elevated. We're talking about taking it up a notch. Everything lives more intensely on the stage. It can't be banal.

The Mai plays herself with the cello towards the end of the play when her dreams have been shattered again, which is a beautiful symbol of futility. How did that come to you?
Well, if you look at the female body it's very like a cello. And the fact that Robert is a musician and that he plays her; it's always been a thing between them. Now she's playing herself, to taunt him. It's a tiny, little fight back, pathetic in a way. She's trying to bring him back in a desperate sort of way. Even when she's fighting him she wants him, which is the whole point of the play. She doesn't leave him. She can't. In every other way she's independent, suc-cessful. She's created this life. She's built this beautiful house. But she's done it all for him. If it weren't for him, she'd be fine, but she believes in princes.

In _Portia Coughlan_ there is a strong sense of the inevitability of fate and in most of your work you explore the idea of predestiny and the haunting of the present by the past. What is it that keeps drawing you back to this theme?
Well, I love the whole Greek idea of tragedy, that it's all uncontrol-lable and that there's a destiny. It's about the journey, rather than the event itself. But I would like to write a play where I don't have to kill off the heroine. I've killed them all off, but I reckon it's aspects of myself that have to be killed off, so I can go on healthier and freer. I was reading an essay of Tennessee Williams's about the tragic sensibility which he says is both within and outside of time.

The way I took it, it doesn't have to be about your life; it's something that's out there and it infects certain people. Some people are drawn to that tragic sensibility, in the way that some people would have a gothic sensibility or a comic sensibility. And the tragic sensibility does appeal to me more. I'm not quite sure why. There's been nothing tragic in my life. I don't know, something about the aesthetic of it. It's beautiful. There's something revealing about it too. There's a discovery in it.

Portia Coughlan **also tackles one of the greatest taboos, in the form of incest between a brother and sister, and the play celebrates this, in many ways, as a greater, higher love. What inspired you to do this? And what particularly fascinated you about the extraordinary relationship between twins?**
It's the double, isn't it? It's the shadow. I would never call it an incest play. I would call it a love relationship between a brother and sister. *On Raftery's Hill* now, the next play, I'd call that an incest play. Well, anything that is taboo is fascinating. It's one of the oldest stories of what the world was born out of, a brother and sister, well, the Greek world, with the tale of Bibylus in Ovid's *Metamorphoses*, where the sister falls in love with her brother.

Was Emily Brontë's *Wuthering Heights* **another influence?**
Oh God, yes. I read that book every year. I love it. It was a huge influence. It's one of my favourite novels. I've read a lot of criticism around it too and I find that people can be very . . . well, in this day and age, because it's emotional, that it's somehow a bit unworthy. I find that really offensive. What's the big deal about controlled emotion? There's some unwritten law that says, 'Don't get emotional, be intellectual!' But I adore that book.

Portia speaks a harsh and cruel truth throughout the play, hiding nothing and sparing no one, in contrast to the others who harbour their terrible secrets. Is it because she faces her own death that she can confront the truth?
I think so, yeah. She's a bit like a savage in the woods. She doesn't lie, but when she does, she lies to point to a bigger truth. But then you're dealing with a disintegrating personality as well. There's no time for anything else, in a sense. She's very afraid too. I think she wants to live, but the shadow is too strong. It's too predestined, too preordained for her to go on. It's too painful. I mean, she says at one point, 'I didn't really like my brother that much when it came right down to it.' It's beyond love. It's some force coming at

her and all she can do is to try and stave it off. She's also mon-
strously selfish, which I really like. It's much more honest. You
can say what you want. And there is a certain relish in her cruelty.
But there's great relish in saying things out even if they are cruel,
if they're true. There's a purity about her. I love her. I can understand why a lot of people don't as well, because I know she's a bit
of a monster. But I love the fight in her, you know? And the
toughness and the meanness. And she's fucking around and she
can't get her act together, but she has a sharper intelligence than
the rest of them. She has a much finer sensibility than they have,
than they're aware of. And they're a bit embarrassed by her. They
want to tell her to 'Shut up and do what you're supposed to do.
Look after the kids and keep the house tidy.' And she says, 'No.
I've tried all that.'

**You wrote *Portia Coughlan* at the National Maternity Hospital
in Dublin. Did this have an impact on what you wrote – the
fact that you were surrounded by birth and babies? And was it
this experience that drove you to turn the tide against the usual
expectations of motherhood and to create a character in Portia
who despises her children?**
I wouldn't say she despises her children. She realises that she can't
love them, which is very different. The fact of writing it at the
Maternity Hospital, I'm sure it did affect me. I didn't want to do
the expected thing. There were lots of reasons, not just to be smart
about it or anything, but it's been done, you know. And it held no
appeal for me.

**There is a tremendous amount of humour as well as a spiritual
and emotional intensity in your work, with highly skilled comic
characterisation – for example, Blaize Scully and Maggie May in
Portia Coughlan. How do you integrate humour so successfully
in a play which is essentially so bleak?**
Well, Patrick Kavanagh, the Irish poet, says that tragedy is under-
developed comedy. There's such a fine line between them. I mean
often tragic events are hilarious, if they're told in a certain way,
with a certain glint or slant on them. And sense of humour is
extremely important to me. If I don't see humour in my work I
know I'm in trouble, because it means there's a lack of lightness of
touch and that's so necessary to playwriting, especially to tragic
playwriting. I think they complement one another wonderfully. I
mean, the whole idea of laughter and tears. They're the same ducts.
There's the same need inside for laughing and crying, the same gut

stuff, the same source. But I was thinking about this, comic touches in tragedy always work, yet tragic touches in comedy rarely do.

The time-frame you use in *Portia Coughlan* is an unusual one in that we see Portia's death and mourn her loss, before witnessing the final days that led up to her suicide. Why did you choose to do this? And what impact did you want it to have on your audience?

Well, it was a formal exercise in one way. I wanted to see how having her die in the middle would affect the third act. I think it works. Playing with time, that interests me. Beyond that, I don't really know. It also served as a focus for gathering the play together. You couldn't actually have Act Two at the end of the play; it wouldn't work. It would be total melodrama. For some strange reason it works where it is. And as I was writing the play I didn't write both the big acts, and then this in the middle. I wrote this and then I wrote Act Three. And after-knowledge of an event that is about to take place always ups the ante.

Your plays show a deep respect for nature and in the case of *The Mai* and *Portia Coughlan* they take place against its powerful backdrop, with Owl Lake and the Belmont River ever-present. Why are these potent images so important to you?

Nature invested with human memory or human association is the kind of nature that fascinates me. With Portia I would say, you talk about the river, but the river is her. It's her and Gabriel. Nature that makes a gratuitous appearance in a play just doesn't interest me, but nature that is invested with memory or nature of character, or associations, faith, is so important. It's another dimension. You're spinning another metaphor, which is feeding into the play.

How difficult is it for you to get work produced in Ireland, given that financial resources are so limited? Does this explain why you have had some of your work produced in England and in the States as well now?

Well, I have managed to get them all produced in Ireland, at the moment, but that may change. England and America I look on as gifts. To get produced at the Royal Court is a huge thing for me and to be produced in America is great as well. I don't know. I see that if there are problems, they're with me. If the work is good enough it'll take care of itself. I really believe in that. Show the work, and if it's good and you've given everything you can to it, it will get put on. It's like a kind of law or something. If you go on about, 'Oh, all these problems,' there always will be. I've had a lot of support. I've been very lucky like that. I know it's a privileged position and I appreciate that. It could all change, of course, in the next five years. They mightn't want to know me. But that's fine too. It's a journey. It's a life journey. It's a lifetime's work. Things are very well for me at the moment, but you read biographies of writers and the real challenge is how to sustain yourself over a lifetime, over a large body of work. And to try to keep getting better and better. Going deeper and deeper. And not writing to please. Writing to please will never sustain you. You might get a couple of plays out of it, but if it's not about yourself, if you're not in it . . . audiences are really perceptive. They pick it up.

Claire Dowie

A maverick writer-performer who developed her own genre, 'stand-up theatre', Claire Dowie started her theatrical career as a dancer, but abandoned this to work as a stand-up comedian when her comedic skills and need to speak out got the better of her. She first started writing and performing her own plays at the suggestion of Colin Watkeys, now her director-producer. Off-beat, straight-up and never missing a joke or a trick, her work exposes hypocrisy at every turn, ridiculing conformity, control and rigid labelling with cool rage, logic and humour. From the tender longings of an emotionally abused child, to the confusions of an adolescent girl growing up in the heady days of Beatlemania, and the hellishness of motherhood, she explores the gamut of human frustrations with integrity and great authenticity, to the point where her plays have often been wrongly mistaken for autobiography.

Claire's brave, brilliant and award-winning work includes: *Adult Child, Dead Child* (which premiered at the Finborough Theatre before touring nationally and won a *Time Out* Award in 1988); *Why is John Lennon Wearing a Skirt?* (first presented at the Traverse Theatre, Edinburgh, and winner of a London Fringe Award in 1991); *Death and Dancing* (BAC, 1992); *Drag Act* (for Gay Sweatshop, Drill Hall and tour, 1993); *Leaking from Every Orifice* (BAC, 1993); *All Over Lovely* (which premiered at the Traverse Theatre as part of the Edinburgh Festival, 1996); and most recently *Easy Access* (for the boys). Her television work includes: *Kevin* (for Central Television) and *Came Out, It Rained, Went Back in Again* (for BBC2's City Shorts season). Her radio work includes: *The Year of the Monkey* (BBC Radio 3). Claire is currently writing a new radio play for the BBC. A volume of her work, WHY IS JOHN LENNON WEARING A SKIRT? AND OTHER STAND-UP THEATRE PLAYS is published by Methuen.

* * *

You term your work very specifically as 'stand-up theatre'. Where did this definition come from?

I hate going to the theatre. I hate seeing plays. They're boring. They don't engage the audience at all. I used to be a stand-up comedian, that's where 'stand-up theatre' comes from. It's like marrying the two. And, you know, if stand-up comedians bomb, they've failed, but actors succeed if they get the job and it's like they don't care what happens after that. They don't pump up their performance if the audience is sitting on its hands. They've got this fourth wall. They're performing in a fish tank.

Why did you leave stand-up comedy to work in theatre?
Because that was boring as well. I don't always want to deliver punchlines. Sometimes I'm in a bad mood. And have you been to comedy shows lately? They're relentlessly dull. People doing this really bland, meaningless garbage just to get some TV producer interested. When I started it was great because you didn't have to be a comedian necessarily, you could just be anything interesting. Then TV got interested and suddenly everybody started gearing their acts towards being acceptable on television. I didn't really want to do theatre as such, but I didn't know what else to do. The only thing I ever liked theatrically was *The Rocky Horror Show*. I saw that years ago and thought, 'That's what I want to do.' But I can't sing. That's the only thing I've ever seen, entertainment-wise, that I thought, 'Wow!' The way they interacted with the audience and told a story, you really got into it. And I thought at first, because I didn't really know much about theatre, that that's what theatre was.

Then I went to see these plays with Colin [Watkeys]. He'd suggested I write a play, and I said, 'Let's go and have a look,' because, you know, I'm working class. And I couldn't believe it. These people poncing around somewhere over there, you know. What's it got to do with me?

Your performance style is very direct and risk-taking. You remove the fourth wall and don't know how an audience will respond. Is it something you thrive on?
Yeah. I don't see it as a risk, though. I just see it as a natural extension of being a comedian. I mean what's going to happen to you? You're going to lose your dignity, your sense of self, your pride, that's about all really. And the performance changes every night, depending on the audience response. That's what makes it interesting. I couldn't do the same thing every day.

You don't rehearse your pieces. How do you prepare?

Just learn them. We rehearsed with Peta [Lily] because *All Over Lovely* was a two-hander, but I don't like rehearsing because you're talking to nobody. You're standing in an empty room and there's nobody there and you feel such a twat. It's like telling a joke to a mirror and expecting the mirror to laugh. It's not going to work. I'm usually a complete wreck on opening night. It's all a leap into the void. I don't even know what I'm going to do and half the time I haven't learnt the script properly, so I've usually got a list in my back pocket, a running order, in case I get stuck and completely forget where the story is supposed to be going. But it's all written down.

Do you discuss things with Colin?
Oh yeah. He directs the script rather than the actual performance. The performance comes from the script. He directs it as it's being written with the view, always, to how it's going to be performed. He's my dramaturg. If I'm writing every day he'll read it all at the end of the day and we'll go through it to see which bits work and which bits don't, and we'll have arguments and shout at each other. And when I perform it, he's there to say whether this works or that works or why the audience didn't like that bit or where I lost them. It's a more organic, ongoing sort of directing than theatre directing.

What do you feel that your type of theatre gives an audience that normal theatre doesn't?
Involvement really. I care about what they think. Proper plays are pat. 'Here it is. Watch it and go home.' If I'm in the audience I think, 'Well what did I contribute?' I didn't. It's all done. It's there. So what? You might as well watch it on telly.

The way you write and what you write about is very potent emotionally. It must produce a strong audience reaction. With *Adult Child, Dead Child* did you get a lot of feedback? Did you get phone calls from psychiatrists?
They talked to me in the bar afterwards. I had one psychiatrist who wouldn't believe it wasn't true. I kept saying, 'It's not true. I made it all up.' He said, 'But the things in it showed it was true.' In the end I just gave up. Colin said there was another psychotherapist in the dressing room saying, 'It's wonderful that she's with her dog now. I'd like to see how she transfers to another human!' There was one night I did it and it was horrible, a really sterile, flat evening. It turned out afterwards about eighty per cent of the

audience were psychologists. You really felt like you were being dissected. It was bizarre.

It did seem really personal, that play. How do you achieve that depth of characterisation?
I just get really interested in the character, in that person. I don't know. *ACDC* came from this woman I met on a train who happened to be a psychiatric nurse and she told me that ninety per cent of patients weren't mental, they just had family problems. You know, it was like the family's fault and that really intrigued me. I thought, 'How awful.' And ages ago there was this kid on a TV programme who'd set fire to his house. He was in a mental hospital for *years* and he wanted to be a magician. It showed you how he was as a kid and how he was ten years later as a grown-up. That was really fascinating because I didn't think he had a problem. I thought his dad did. That started me off as well.

Do you do research?
No. Colin does that. I work on the person and how logically that person would react, you know, how I would react. If this happened to me, how would I feel emotionally? I get totally fascinated. You get overtaken by it in a way, so obsessed that nothing else is important. But it's not so much that I become the character, I just take on their history. I'm still me, I just change my history.

How much of your own experience did you draw on, for example, in *Why is John Lennon Wearing a Skirt?* And did you consciously set out to explore the issue of female conditioning?
It was a whole lot of things. When I was at school I was obsessively anti-skirt. I thought, 'What's the point of these things?' I hated the skirt. Even now, when I'm taking Rachel [*Claire's daughter*] around I've noticed that little two- and three-year-old girls are for some reason wearing really long dresses. Have you seen them trying to play in them? They keep tripping over and falling down. They're being conditioned to think they can't do it. It's not occurring to them that it's their clothes. They're going to grow up thinking they can't climb trees and they can't run around or go on the slide because their dresses have stopped them. I was obsessed with that when I was a schoolkid and that sort of came back when I also heard about this black woman who was convinced she was white. Nobody could convince her otherwise. She had pictures of her 'family' – she'd just cut out pictures of white people from a magazine. That was her way of reacting to racism. Racism was so bad

she just rejected it. With the *John Lennon* character it was misogyny. She was rejecting being female. But I did have a gang. I was one of the Beatles, so there was a lot of experience in it, I suppose. And I never start with an issue. I start with the character.

In all your work, patriarchal society comes under attack, but in *Death and Dancing* you also draw attention to the misogyny within the male, gay world. Do you think woman is still the 'nigger of the world'?
I think women do it to themselves half the time. I include women in that patriarchal society that I hate. The thing with *Death and Dancing* and the gay and lesbian world is that . . . Oh, they make me angry because they're halfway there! They're halfway to seeing the complete scam that civilisation is. They don't need to play that game, yet they do. They play the whole status quo. They could change it! Instead they're trying to fit into it. Why? Why? If you're not allowing yourself to be conditioned sexually, why are you allowing yourself to be conditioned culturally? That's how I feel about women as well. Why do they put up with it? Even with something like *John Lennon* some women get really angry because you're pointing out to them where they've been coerced and they blame me for it. It's threatening to them and they're sitting there pulling down their short skirts. I don't know why people get so angry with me. I point things out. I don't mean to be threatening.

Do you think things are getting any better?
No, which is where I'm am at the moment with this latest play *All Over Lovely*. I've got this new bee in my bonnet about, 'Has feminism done anything at all?' Or is it just economics? We say women have got all this freedom, but when you really look at it, it's simply that women are cheap slave labour. I'm not really there yet. I think I wrote the play too early. What would feminism or women be if we had pursued what we really are, rather than what men have got? We slotted ourselves into the patriarchal thing, you know, 'I want to have a job. I want to be a man.' Everyone wants to be a white, middle-class, heterosexual male. I've never totally agreed with feminists. I agree with feminism, I just don't agree with the crap that's spouted in the name of it. I've always had a problem with it. Now I'm getting quite acceptable because everyone else is getting disillusioned with feminism. I've never blamed men for women's predicament and I've had an awful lot of arguments about that. My argument's always been that women are not stupid, so how on earth did they get themselves into the position where

they're unable to do whatever they want to do? There must be collusion. There must be. Women can get together and stop whatever they want to stop, really. It's institutions I have a problem with and feminism has become an institution. It's become middle-class women telling working-class women what they should be doing, and working-class women can't do it because they don't have the freedoms of middle-class women.

Do you think it has got more to do with the economy than anything else?
It's all to do with the economy.

So would you have more in common with socialist feminists?
Yeah, but socialism is economy again. I'm a Luddite actually. I think we should go back to pre-industrial revolution. Blow up the computers and get rid of money.

Tell us more!
Ooh, ooh, a teapot revolution! (*She laughs.*) It makes no sense to me. This idea of having to earn a living. It's bizarre if you think about it. You have no right to a living, you have to *earn* it.

Do you want to change people's minds? Is that one of the reasons you write?
Yes. All right, let's get down to it. I want to rule the world. I want to be God. Yes. I want to change the world. But I don't think theatre can do that. My audience are the ones who agree with me predominantly. I'm just one of those people who says what they're thinking. It's a generational thing, the hippy thing. How did everyone suddenly become hippies? It's evolution.

You've nearly always written work to fulfil your own performance needs, but more recently you have written plays for other people. Does this mean you take yourself more seriously as a writer now? And is it strange to lose control over your work?
I haven't lost control over anything yet except my bladder when I cough! I'm writing stuff because I can't perform anymore, not with Rachel at the moment, and I keep saying, 'Well next year, when she's four, she might be old enough to sit and watch the shows without shouting, "What are you doing mummy?" ' But, of course, I'll have another one by then. That's the only reason I'm writing for other people. And it's enjoyable. Plus the fact that I'm more confident now that I am a 'writer'. For years I wouldn't say I was

a writer. I carried on saying I was a stand-up comedian. And I'm severely limited in doing shows about forty-year-old women. There's only so much you can say really, so it's nice to write other things.

And how do you feel about women's position in theatre?
They're marginalised and dismissed; when it comes to men judging women. Men judge men hoping they'll succeed, whereas with women it's, 'Let's see you fail.' Michael Billington has never been to see any of my work. Maybe he still thinks I'm a comedian. He's still glorying in the days when he went to see *Look Back in Anger*. He wouldn't get it if he did come!

Naomi Wallace

Naomi Wallace is a Kentucky-born poet and playwright whose work has been predominantly staged in Britain, where her rise to recognition and main-stage production has been meteoric. Her first play, *The War Boys*, was presented at the Finborough Theatre in 1993, where she was lauded for, among other things, storming 'traditional male preserves by writing about a wholly male experience' (*Time Out*). This was followed by *In the Heart of America*, a tender, erotic and angry response to the racism and xenophobia engendered by the Gulf War (Bush Theatre, 1994); her highly accomplished play *One Flea Spare*, set during the Great Plague in 1665 (Bush Theatre, 1995); *Slaughter City* (which premiered at the Royal Shakespeare Company's Pit in 1996); and *Birdy*, an adaptation of William Wharton's anti-war novel, which opened in the West End in March 1997. American theatre finally woke up to her talent earlier this year when *One Flea Spare* was staged at the Public Theatre, New York – Naomi's first US production.

Examining oppression and injustice at every turn, her work is refreshingly subversive, humorous and political, raising fundamental questions about the constructs which have created and conditioned our beliefs and behaviour, in the endeavour to reclaim more of our humanity. But she avoids empty rhetoric and sloganising through an inspired use of language, in which unusual metaphor, poetry and myth are at the heart of her engaging explorations.

Naomi is currently working on a new play, *Tressel at Pope Lick Creek* and is co-writing a film with Bruce McLean. *Slaughter City* and *Birdy* appear in single text editions published by Faber & Faber, who also publish *One Flea Spare* in BUSH THEATRE PLAYS. Naomi lives in Iowa City.

* * *

What prompted you to have so much of your work produced in Britain? Are you disillusioned with American theatre as well as American society?

It was simply where my first show landed and I feel terribly warmly inclined towards any country that wants to do my work! The facts are that the British do produce a slightly larger percentage of women and there's an open tradition of political theatre in Britain, so perhaps they were more receptive to my work initially, although I feel that it's too early to say that really. I've received rough rides in Britain as well, in terms of the reception of my work. There's been some controversy about it and I did recently come across a statistic that in 1996, of the 240 productions reviewed by the *Sunday Times* only twenty-eight of them were by women, which is appalling. There's a lot to be done in terms of getting women's work produced.

Am I disillusioned with American theatre? I haven't really been involved with American theatre. My first show opened in New York at the Public only very recently: *One Flea Spare*, which was commissioned by the Bush Theatre. Disillusioned? No, I'm not disillusioned with anything. I'm excited to engage and debate and have my work out there. I think disillusion is a real privilege and I'm not interested in sitting back and being sour.

You started your creative life as a poet and your poetic use of language comes through very clearly in your plays. How much has it helped your playwriting and what made you decide to switch your attention to drama? Did you feel that you needed a more public forum to debate your ideas?
I still consider myself a poet. But one of the reasons I was drawn to the theatre was because writing poetry is such a private enterprise and over the past few years I did begin to feel that I wanted to collaborate. My work is at its best when it is influenced by others. And theatre is a more public forum. The art itself is experienced in a community and I like that. Theatre is also more open to political ideas. But sometimes I will write a poem on an area of interest that is going to become a play. I wrote a poem called 'Meatstrike' before I began work on *Slaughter City*. It's helpful in that I distil the idea down to like twenty lines and then sometimes parts of that poem will go into the play, although usually it's later cut out.

Issues are clearly at the heart of your work and you are a very political writer. How do you transform your ideas into a dramatic and creative text?
It's a long process. When I wrote *Slaughter City* I thought, 'There's very little that's been put on stage about labour struggles, more maybe in the 1930s, but how do you do that again now in a vital

and dramatic way?' When you're dealing with labour issues there's a certain rhetoric that you can't get away from, so my challenge was, 'How do I take this rhetoric and make it come alive again so people hear it, hear these issues again?' It's usually something specific that draws me to write. With *Slaughter City* I happened to be living in Kentucky at the time and I would drive by this meat-packing plant and see these people. They'd be covered in blood from the work they were doing, dangerous work, and I thought, 'What must it be like to spend most of your waking life up to your knees in blood and be paid hell's wages for it?' With *In the Heart of America* it took me a while to even start research because I was so angry about the Gulf War and about the false information that American culture gave to its people about that war.

I was also very attracted, at a sensual level, to the names of the weaponry, to the names of the bombs, and I began to think, 'Well what does that mean? We've used this language to make beautiful something that is so destructive. This language of destruction is being presented as a language of love and what does that mean?' The main objective of war is to protect the body on the one hand and to destroy the body on the other. And a lot of the time my interest does centre around the body, the body's place in history and what happens to the body in a certain set of social circumstances.

In *The War Boys* you expose the American dream as empty, divisive and illusory. What were your reasons for writing this play?
I've always been interested in how mainstream culture influences us in very intimate ways. I think, in American culture, we under-estimate how much it influences how we see ourselves and how we see others. In its representation of both men and women it deforms or perverts our sexuality. Men must behave in a certain way: straight, white and macho, and women must behave in a certain way. We like think that we're beyond that, that we're above culture somehow, but when we grow up as children there's no way of escaping it. We don't have defences against that, so coming to consciousness about an exploitative culture, a sexist culture, takes some time. Some damage has already been done to all of us who grow up in a capitalist, sexist or racist culture. I wanted to show that in *The War Boys*.

I was rereading an essay by Edward Bond, called 'On Violence'. What I specifically appreciate about it is how he sees culture as a very active and brutalising force. We tend to see violence only in terms of war or crime. The daily violence that's inflicted on the majority of people in a capitalist country is almost invisible: 'This is what your body's supposed to be. This is the size it's supposed to be. This is the way it's supposed to love. This is the way your desire must be directed.' We spend most of our lives trying to deconstruct a vision of ourselves that was imposed on us. But I do believe in complete possibility for both men and women. We are taught to become men and we are taught to become women and therein lies the hope that we can teach ourselves to become different kinds of men and women.

In *The War Boys* you make a clear link between the dysfunctional backgrounds of David, Greg and George, and the brutality they exercise as adults in the Light Up the Border Brigade, showing how misplaced their rage is and how their racism stems from self-hatred and their own victimisation. Do you think this area has been too little explored?

In terms of American theatre there's been a tremendous amount on dysfunctional families. I'm interested in making a link between a dysfunctional family and a dysfunctional society. There's this idea that the family is where it all starts and that if the family goes wrong messed-up people are sent out into society and they then mess up society. I think it's the other way round. We've got a society that in some ways is destructive towards the family, because the family structure is heterosexual and usually sexist and that's what's accepted in society. What I'm trying to do with my new play *Tressel at Pope Lick Creek* is to present two families, decent families, who struggle against becoming destroyed through poverty, through violence outside the family: the violence of society. A lot of people don't want to accept that poverty is a system of violence, that people have to live with violence on a daily basis. It's not visible. You don't have money to clothe your children properly or to pay your bills. It's a violence that has the continual possibility of erupting because of the tremendous stress of survival.

Capitalist society is dysfunctional for the majority of us. It's a system that provides only for a minority. That we don't all turn out monsters is a miracle. The codes that many of us have been forced to live by are destructive. They are not codes that make us bigger or more generous people. They are actually inhuman. But to question those or to consider that there might be an alternative is deemed idiocy, naiveté or both, so in some senses my work is unfashionable. And it's great to be unfashionable, but it can also keep people from doing your work. Hopefully that's changing, though.

How do you feel about the acclaim you won regarding *The War Boys* for 'the daring way she storms traditional male preserves by writing about a wholly male experience'?

Women did not write about certain things because for a long time we were not supposed to write about war, about male preserves. There's such absurdity in that. The idea is that human experience, 'universal' experience, is usually white, male and straight. That has been accepted as all our experience and, of course, it's not. At the same time, writing is an act of imagination. What am I going to do? Only write plays about the experience of white women? That doesn't interest me. If you're creating a character you're already going out of your experience, whether you're a man or a woman or someone of a different age. Some of the greatest novels on war were by men who hadn't even been to war. For ourselves as women there shouldn't be anything we can't write about. That's why I do a lot of research. I figure if I'm writing out of my experience I'd better know about as much as I can and stay open to criticism.

One of the recurring explorations in your work is the import- ance of the human body and how it has been devalued, degraded and even destroyed. What do you find so compelling about this exploration?

The body is our home and the power of culture to make us feel not at home in what should be our home has always fascinated me. In a patriarchal culture women in general are made to feel dissatis- fied with their bodies, to hate their bodies, sometimes to the point of starvation or suicide. Our bodies have become our enemy in a sense. They don't match up to what the culture says they should. That is the trick of the culture, to make us dissatisfied with what is ours, to make us feel powerless, because when you are unhappy with what you have, you do feel powerless. Not only does capi- talism encourage the dissatisfaction we constantly have with our bodies, but by not seeing our bodies as powerful, we are also incapable of seeing them as agents of change.

And I've always been interested in the way that the body is used up and broken down through labour. Our bodies do break down through age, that's part of the natural process, but in this economic system, the labour and use is sucked out and when the body breaks down it's thrown aside and replaced with new labour. To me that's completely inhuman. People are treated as disposable, and Social Security in this country [the USA] is pitiful. Most people are just swept to the side and they live in poverty till the day they die. It's a terrible injustice. At the end of our lives, having given our labour willingly, we should have peace, quiet and safety and that's not the end of the road for most of us.

It's unusual to explore with tenderness an elderly woman's sexuality, as you do with Darcy in *One Flea Spare*. Did you want to reclaim the sexuality of women whom society no longer values?
You know, I'm not a teenager anymore and I can see, not only from my own experience but in general, that the older we get the less value we have. In a culture that's all about exchange value, we get to a certain age and we're no longer seen as being able to produce children, our labour is not much good, we're no longer considered desirous and we're dead from the neck down. Our desire and sexuality doesn't die, but we live in a culture that says, 'You can't be sexual and you can't have desire. And if you do, we'll make it invisible or tell you you're a dirty old woman.' Cultures such as the American Indian culture see you as *more* valuable as you get older; your life is cumulative and you're considered wiser. I just thought, 'What a shame that in mainstream society our lives aren't cumulative.' We're seen as diminishing people, whereas really we are becoming enriched and that's what should be recognised. We may be shrinking in our bodies, but our experience has grown and our knowledge has grown. That's something our society should invest in. And with Darcy I did want to put a woman on stage who is complex in her sexuality at a much older age, to show that at sixty-five you can be just as complicated as you are at twenty, if not perhaps more so.

In *One Flea Spare* you use the Plague and the unusual restrictions it placed on people to expose the unnatural hierarchy and roles society normally imposes. The characters are forced to renegotiate their relationships and discover new identities. What compelled you to explore this and do you think we as a human race have lost touch with our common humanity?
Issues of power – who has it, how power is negotiated and what that does to us – have always fascinated me. Some people have said that they find my work very dark, that there's not much hope in it, but I see my work as irresponsibly hopeful. I think it's through engaging with the struggles of power that suddenly there comes a moment where there's a possibility for transformation. With *One Flea Spare* I tried to highlight those moments of possibility, not to give a happy ending and say we've changed these structures of power, which are very difficult to change and sometimes only

change for a short period of time, but instead to show the possibility of changing or disturbing them.

Have we lost touch with our common humanity? If anyone's lost their humanity it's those who rule our country. But what always surprises me in studying history and trying to become aware of social forces, is how much humanity and dignity is retained under terrible forces of destruction or oppression. We always find ways to keep our humanity alive. Humanity has survived and that is what continues to challenge what oppresses it. The majority of us have not lost touch.

In *Slaughter City* the relationship between Cod and the Sausage-maker is a powerful metaphor for how the relationship between capital and labour has been defined through post-industrial history. Yet by the end of the play Cod has managed, in part at least, to reclaim her power and subvert expectation of the inevitable. Was it important for you to make this relationship symbolic – something which exists out of time, to show how even the powerful swing of history can be changed and does not necessarily have to repeat itself?

We often feel that we are victims of history as opposed to agents of it. People say history repeats itself, well that's a real comfortable thing for those who are in power, for those who enjoy the luxuries of this society, because what it's really saying is, 'Don't try to change anything because it's going to repeat itself anyway.' Certain structures of power do repeat themselves, but those structures have also been torn down by history again and again. The fact is we're living now and the idea that nothing really changes is there to protect those in power, so that the majority will sit back and say, 'I guess this is our lot. It's fate,' like those who say, 'Well there's always rich and poor. It will always be that way.' That's comforting to a minority.

It hasn't always been that way. There have been times in history when things have been more egalitarian, when men and women have been valued equally. It has happened before and it can certainly happen again. But it was difficult to create Cod and the Sausage-maker because how do you make something a metaphor but still enable them to be characters in their own right? It's a delicate balance.

Your plays' time schemes are far from linear, with events switching back and forth from past to present. As a poet this structure must interest you anyway, but do you also use it

because linear structures are reactionary and reinforce inevitability?

There was a time when I believed that linear structures were inherently oppressive, but having seen work that is completely non-linear, completely avant-garde and yet has the most reactionary politics, I don't go for that anymore. There are some things to be said for Aristotelian drama and how it reinforces order and does away with resistance. There is a certain truth to some of that because a lot of the work was written to support the order at the time. But for me, what I like about non-linear time schemes is that I've always felt that not only is the past not over, but that the present is also history. History is always rupturing the present. It's just a matter of recognising that and realising that in order to change our future we have to deal with our past. What I love about theatre is that you can have three-dimensional time visible on stage in a way that you can't in other media. That's really exciting to me.

Slaughter City **also examines the issues of gender and race oppression as part of its more central analysis of the power struggle between capital and labour. Do you feel very strongly that all forms of oppression derive from the same thing; that sexism, racism and anti-gay prejudice are all symptoms of the capitalist system?**

I do believe that all oppressions are linked to the inequalities and divisive nature of capitalism. Capitalism thrives on inequality and keeping people divided and I'm interested in how this oppression functions and where and how we can challenge it. I've been thinking a lot lately about the term 'feminist'. The sad thing is that a lot of women have been terrified into staying away from this word, 'I'm not a feminist, but . . .' and I think it's important for us to defend the gains of feminism and to also say that it has influenced our work. At the same time, I think to only speak about women's oppression is a mistake. Capitalism adapts and it is possible to envision a capitalist system where women would have equal pay but where you'd still have an upper class and a working class. And what have we got then? An upper-class woman gets the same pay, as a man so that she can hire a maid to clean her floor? I think capitalism could also adapt at some point to become a free place for gays and lesbians. It's not inconceivable that gay liberation could become compatible with capitalism. That's why we need to make these links between sexual, gender and economic oppression. Capitalism is very good at adapting, at disguising its lie, and we need to keep that in mind.

Your writing is courageous, confrontational and strong in its ability to draw together similar themes and issues which society chooses to ignore or view as totally separate. You make links, for example, between racism and war, and in *In the Heart of America* you force audiences to see that the malaise is everywhere. Do you see your main task as a playwright to open eyes and wake people up?

Well, they damn well better be awake. I'd hate for them to be falling asleep at my work! I've never seen my work as something to give people answers. I've always seen my challenge to get people to see something in a new way. To disturb, yes, that's what I'd like my work to do, but to disturb them in a way that they would come back for more. I think questioning is what really moves us forward. I make these links because, like I said, I don't believe in the singularity of oppression. When you see how closely racism and war are linked and how one country dehumanises another in order to make the killing acceptable to the entire country! It's what we did with the Iraqis. They became acceptable targets for the hi-tech war. That was one reason why the media coverage of the carnage was absolutely nil, to the great discredit of most mainstream news agencies. I hope that lies heavy on their conscience because it was a real tragedy. The United States cultivates amnesia, to forget what's happened, because to accept the past terrifies those in power. The racism that arose during the Gulf War was horrific. People in different parts of the USA were beaten to death; Indians mistaken for Arabs, Arabs mistaken for this and that. Racism and xenophobia are nurtured during a time of war, so that our conscience is clear for the killing. I felt it was important to challenge that in *In the Heart of America*, which I hope I did to some extent.

What attracted you to creating a stage adaptation of William Wharton's novel *Birdy*?

I was asked to do that adaptation and I liked William Wharton's novel a lot. It was an anti-war novel and he also made links between war and the oppression of young men, as men, in our culture; the way in which war machines are built up, even during peacetime, in the male psyche. Young men are also destroyed through sexism. It's important to recognise that, because feminism has often presented sexism as something that is mainly to do with women, but I think that men, even straight men, are also influenced by the rigidity of what's considered to be sexually normal. I chose to foreground Wharton's themes a little further by talking about an intimate friendship between two men that in some ways flies in the face of traditional male bonding, the way men are expected to behave in male friendships and how they deal with intimacy.

Your progress and recognition as a playwright in the UK has been rapid, taking you from the Finborough to the RSC and now to the West End in just five plays. What does this success mean to you?
I'm interested in engaging and challenging mainstream culture and you need to be out there in order to be able to do that. Even if a lot of people do not like my work, they have to recognise and deal with it and I'm glad about that. No one likes shouting in the dark. I'll shout in the dark if I have to, but I do want to challenge the mainstream, and what recognition has given me, is an opportunity to do that. The reception of my work has not always been warm, of course. But I'm glad my work's getting done. I'm glad it has this opportunity. I just hope it will carry on for a few more years.